CAMBRIDGE MUSIC HANDBOOKS

Mozart: Clarinet Concerto

CAMBRIDGE MUSIC HANDBOOKS

GENERAL EDITOR Julian Rushton

Cambridge Music Handbooks provide accessible introductions to major musical works, written by the most informed commentators in the field.

With the concert-goer, performer and student in mind, the books present essential information on the historical and musical context, the composition, and the performance and reception history of each work, or group of works, as well as critical discussion of the music.

Other published titles

Mozart: Clarinet Concerto

Colin Lawson

CAMBRIDGE
UNIVERSITY PRESS

Published by the Press Syndicate of the University of Cambridge
The Pitt Building, Trumpington Street, Cambridge CB2 1RP
40 West 20th Street, New York, NY 10011–4211, USA
10 Stamford Road, Oakleigh, Melbourne 3166, Australia

First published 1996

Printed in Great Britain at the University Press, Cambridge

A catalogue record for this book is available from the British Library

Library of Congress cataloguing in publication data
Lawson, Colin (Colin James)
Mozart, clarinet concerto / Colin Lawson
p. cm. – (Cambridge music handbooks)
Includes bibliographical references and index.
ISBN 0 521 47384 5 (hardback) – ISBN 0 521 47929 0 (paperback).
1. Mozart, Wolfgang Amadeus, 1756–1791. Concertos, clarinet, orchestra, K.622, A major.
I. Title. II Series.
ML410.M9L26 1996
784.2'862–dc20 95–22790 CIP MN

ISBN 0 521 47384 5 hardback
ISBN 0 521 47929 0 paperback

AH

Contents

Contents

Illustrations

Preface

As appreciation of Mozart's music becomes ever more widespread, it seems natural that his final instrumental work should prove a particular source of fascination and delight; indeed, the popularity of the Clarinet Concerto has undoubtedly never been greater. Not surprisingly, scholars of Mozart's style and language have subjected the Concerto to close analysis with a view to speculating as to the directions Mozart might have taken had he achieved a normal life-span. Even a mere ten years after its composition it was already recognised by at least one reviewer as a masterpiece and 'the foremost clarinet concerto in the world'.[1] Few today would dissent from this judgement, notwithstanding some formidable later competition from Weber, Spohr, Nielsen and Copland, amongst others. Above all, the work represents a triumphant manifestation of the widespread eighteenth-century desire to appeal both to amateurs of music and to connoisseurs.

Mozart's association with the clarinettist Anton Stadler radically advanced the profile of the instrument and its idiomatic potential. The Concerto marks the culmination of a century of quite astonishing activity in the history of the clarinet following its development in the years around 1700. A persistent myth that the clarinet began with Mozart has been finally laid to rest by some illuminating recent research into the early eighteenth-century instrument and its music, which has served to enhance rather than to diminish appreciation of his achievement.[2] There were some idiomatic solo compositions by Vivaldi, Handel, Johann and Carl Stamitz and a number of others, but no one understood the clarinet so well as Mozart. It is indeed good fortune for posterity that he should have encountered a virtuoso such as Stadler, that Vienna was at the forefront of developments in clarinet manufacture and that the instrument itself had recently reached a state of technical development which made it an ideal vehicle for Mozart's musical inspiration.

The autograph score of the Concerto is lost and it survives only in early nineteenth-century editions. This is particularly regrettable because the work was written for a new clarinet specially developed by Stadler, whose range was

Ex. 1

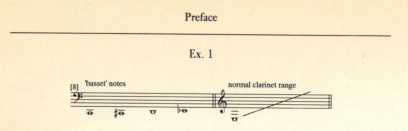

extended downwards by four semitones to include the low tonic of its fundamental scale. Now known as the basset clarinet, this is the kind of instrument increasingly used today in concerts and recordings, enabling Mozart's melodic contours to be realised in what approaches their original form. The Concerto was composed for clarinet in A, whose notes sound a minor third lower than written, as in all the musical illustrations from the work which follow. The extra low notes were notated by Mozart an octave below pitch, as shown above (Ex. 1).

At present we cannot be certain of every detail of Mozart's original score, though some useful aids exist for reconstructing the text, such as the autograph sketch K621b of the Concerto's first 199 bars, as well as some musical illustrations contained within a review of an early edition. During the last fifty years some eminent players and scholars have published valuable further suggestions, including George Dazeley (1948), Jiří Kratochvíl (1956), Ernst Hess (1967), Alan Hacker (1969) and Pamela Poulin (1977). The *Neue Mozart-Ausgabe* (1977) published versions of the Concerto for both normal and basset clarinet, together with a useful piano reduction.[3] The current climate of historical performance has encouraged adherence to Mozart's original slurs and other surface detail, recognising that it was largely through these devices that his expressive intent was relayed. The *NMA* allows access to this information from the best available sources, with editorial suggestions clearly differentiated. The myriad of other editions – many by highly distinguished clarinettists – are generally more interventionist, some requiring careful interpretation.[4]

It is a pleasure to thank a large number of friends for their help, advice and inspiration in the preparation of this book. A powerful catalyst was initially supplied by the Cambridge maker Daniel Bangham, who in 1988 produced for me a wonderfully responsive boxwood basset clarinet of his own design. I am especially grateful to Caroline Brown, artistic director of The Hanover Band, for many subsequent opportunities to explore the richness of the Concerto in period performance. Like all students of clarinet history, I owe a special debt to Nicholas Shackleton, who during the gestation of this project was (as usual) generous enough to place at my disposal his unrivalled knowledge of surviving instruments worldwide. Eric Hoeprich kindly provided for publication two photographs of instruments from his own collection. Albert Rice also showed characteristic kindness in sharing important information about relevant instruments and repertoire for inclusion within the appendices. In addition, I was delighted to have William McColl's permission to reproduce his translation of the 1802 review of the first Breitkopf and Härtel edition of the Concerto.

My wife Hilary has made many perspicacious comments about details in the text and has given the project a great deal of encouragement, despite the fact that its development has entailed long periods of absence at the word-processor, even throughout normal bouts of concert preparation and the usual frantic searches for a playable clarinet reed. Lastly, I must extend my sincere thanks to Penny Souster and her team at Cambridge University Press for their helpful advice and firm but unobtrusive guidance in bringing the book to fruition.

In the following chapters, pitch registers are indicated in the usual manner: middle C just below the treble staff is indicated as c', with each successive octave higher shown as c'', c''', c'''' etc. and the octave below as c, the lowest written pitch of the basset clarinet. Bar numbers within the Concerto are prefaced by an indication of the movement in which they appear, e.g. 1/1, 3/353.

The eighteenth-century clarinet and its music

Origins and birth of the clarinet

It is a remarkable fact that little more than a hundred years before the composition of Mozart's Clarinet Concerto K622, there had yet been no inclusion of single-reed instruments in art music. Despite a long history in folk music, no evidence of clarinet-types in written scores occurs until just before 1700, and this accounts for the clarinet's reputation as the youngest member of the orchestral wind section. In fact, the baroque flute, oboe and bassoon had been developed not many years before, and were featured in the orchestra by Lully (1632–87); however, these instruments were more closely related to their antecedents, both in design and in musical usage.

The early years of the clarinet are especially relevant to a study of Mozart's Concerto, because the principal registers featured and contrasted so effectively within its solo part existed for many years as two distinctive instruments. The starting point for any discussion of the birth of the chalumeau and the clarinet remains J. G. Doppelmayr's *Historische Nachricht von den Nürnbergischen Mathematicis und Kunstlern* (Nuremberg, 1730), whose biography of the maker Johann Christoph Denner (1655–1707) contains the celebrated statement: 'At the beginning of the current century, he invented a new kind of pipe-work, the so-called clarinet, to the great delight of all music-lovers, discovered again from ancient times the already well-known stick or rackett bassoon, and at length presented an improved chalumeau'. It has been observed that Doppelmayr is elsewhere not always a wholly reliable source, that he tended to exaggerate the achievements of local craftsmen and that he failed to assess the contributions of other makers to the development of the chalumeau and clarinet.[1] But the most serious problem is his failure to make clear the relationship of the two instruments and Denner's involvement with each. Nevertheless, no evidence has emerged to contradict Doppelmayr's claim, which finds support in other sources such as Bonanni's *Gabinetto armonico* (Rome, 1722), Walther's *Musicalisches Lexicon* (Leipzig, 1732) and Majer's *Museum musicum* (Schwäbisch Hall, 1732).

These sources describe a two-keyed chalumeau with recorder footjoint resembling a specimen by Denner which survives in Munich. Its mouthpiece and bore were designed to produce effectively a fundamental range of an eleventh or twelfth. Majer identified a family of soprano, alto or quart, tenor and bass chalumeaux, which were hard to blow because of their difficult embouchure. Musical sources show that Majer's four chalumeaux corresponded in length to sopranino, descant, treble and tenor recorders, though sounding an octave lower on account of the acoustical properties of the cylindrical stopped pipe. Majer noted that the fingerings closely correspond with those of the recorder, and it seems likely that this was the instrument which gave rise to the chalumeau, perhaps during attempts to increase its dynamic range.

On the other hand, Bonanni's clarinet (*clarone*) was two-and-a-half palms long, terminating in a trumpet-like bell three inches in width, and with a further differentiating feature from the chalumeau: its two key-holes were no longer diametrically opposite; instead, the thumb-key hole was further towards the mouthpiece, as with the modern speaker key. On Bonanni's evidence, it would be possible to take Doppelmayr's ambiguous statement at face value; perhaps Denner extended the range of the chalumeau and then proceeded to develop the clarinet by means of a smaller mouthpiece and re-sited speaker key, projecting its characteristic upper register via a bell rather than a mere recorder-type footjoint. Bonanni described its sound as high and vigorous, whilst significantly Majer and Walther observed that from afar it sounded like a trumpet, a characterisation nicely reflected in the earliest clarinet repertoire. Two-keyed clarinets in C and in D by Denner's son Jacob survive in Berlin, Brussels and Nuremberg.[2]

Walther and Majer ascribed the invention of the clarinet to a Nuremberger 'at the beginning of this century', information which patently derives from Doppelmayr, and suggests an air of uncertainty even in the 1730s. There is a long tradition of writings which specifically mention the date of 1690 or thereabouts, an early example being C. G. Murr's *Beschreibung der vornehmsten Sehenswürdigkeiten in Nürnberg* (Nuremberg, 1778). Recent research has unearthed various references to the chalumeau from this time; for example, 'Ein Chor Chalimo von 4. Stücken' was purchased from Nuremberg in 1687 for the Duke of Römhild-Sachsen, according to Herbert Heyde's 1976 catalogue of the wind instruments at the Bachhaus in Eisenach.[3] Usage of the chalumeau in Germany is documented from shortly afterwards in an anonymous collection now in Darmstadt, inscribed 'Hannover 1690' and entitled 'XII^c Concert Charivari ou nopce de village a 4 Violon, 2 Chalumeaux

3 Pollissons et un Tambour les Viollons en Vielle'. In an autobiographical sketch Telemann observed that during his career at Hildesheim (1697–1701) he became acquainted with the oboe, flute, 'Schalümo' and gamba, amongst other instruments. Furthermore, it is significant that in 1696 J. C. Denner and the woodwind maker Johann Schell successfully petitioned the Nuremberg city council to be recognised as master craftsmen and to be granted permission to make for sale the '. . . French musical instruments . . . which were invented about twelve years ago [i.e. in 1684] in France'. Whilst the document specifies only recorder and oboe, it is surely not unreasonable to surmise that the single-reed chalumeau was also one of the new instruments.[4] Earliest documentary evidence of the clarinet post-dates the development of the chalumeau by some years. A 1710 invoice for instruments ordered from Jacob Denner for the Duke of Gronsfeld in Nuremberg includes besides chalumeaux '2 Clarinettes' – the first known reference to the clarinet in any source.

Repertoire for chalumeau and two-keyed clarinet

The chalumeau repertoire is extensive and varied, with contributions from a number of pre-eminent German composers, including Fasch, Graupner and Telemann.[5] Handel, Vivaldi and Molter were among other composers who were acquainted with both chalumeau and clarinet and clearly differentiated their idioms. However, it is the long Viennese tradition of writing for the chalumeau which bears directly upon a study of Mozart. The instrument was used as early as the first decade of the century, took part in the Vienna versions of Gluck's *Orfeo* (1762) and *Alceste* (1767), and survived into the 1770s. The soprano chalumeau (range $f - bb''$ or c''') became a favourite obbligato colour, notably in operas and oratorios written between 1708 and 1728 by the court Kapellmeister Johann Joseph Fux (1660–1741).[6] The chalumeau generally appears as an alternative to the oboe in pastoral or love scenes, either in pairs or with the flute or recorder; this distinction between the character of double and single reeds nicely anticipates Mozart's treatment of the woodwinds (and prominent clarinet writing) in *Così fan tutte*. Significantly, Köchel's biography of Fux (Vienna, 1872) cites two references written by the composer in 1718 and 1721 for court oboists who also played the chalumeau. From 1706 until the 1730s the soprano chalumeau made regular obbligato appearances in the works of contemporaries such as Ariosti, Bonno, the brothers Bononcini, Caldara, Conti, Porsile and Reutter; the Emperor Joseph I wrote an aria with chalumeau obbligato for insertion in Ziani's opera *Chilonida* (1709). In 1707 an amusing vignette finds a place in the libretto to Bononcini's *L'Etearco*, written for the Vienna carnival that year. During Act III an exchange takes place between two comic characters, in which the remark, 'I'll try to find both bassoons and oboes', is met with the retort, 'I'd like there to be chalumeaux as well'. Thus the chalumeau was perceived as an attractive novelty, to be distinguished from the traditional woodwinds.

No evidence of the chalumeau in Vienna during the 1740s and 1750s has yet come to light, so the circumstances of Gluck's revival remain something of a mystery. The list of court players compiled by Köchel reveals the survival into old age of oboists who must have known the instrument and perhaps were in a position to influence pupils. Repertoire with chalumeau from the 1770s includes ballets by Aspelmayr (1728–86) and Starzer (1726–87), as well as Gassmann's late opera *I rovinati*. The first known appearance in Vienna of the clarinettist brothers Anton and Johann Stadler was in 1773, but around this time divertimenti with chalumeau were still being composed by the generation of Dittersdorf (1739–99), Gassmann (1729–74) and Pichl (1741–1805). Above all, the concerto by Hoffmeister (1754–1812) testifies to the ability of a native virtuoso even at this late stage. Viennese enthusiasm for the chalumeau at the threshold of the classical period has never been fully explained, but is confirmed in a magnificent if belated tribute by Daniel Schubart, whose *Ideen zu einer Ästhetik der Tonkunst* (written in 1784–5 but published only in 1806) observes: 'its tone is so interesting, individual and endlessly pleasant, that the whole world of music would suffer a grievous loss if the instrument ever fell into disuse'.[7] It is certainly true that the sound of the chalumeau can never be reproduced even on a clarinet of Mozart's day, though the limited compass made its demise inevitable once the clarinet became fluent in both its principal registers.

A tenuous if important link exists between Mozart and the chalumeau. This relates to a 'Musica da Cammera' by Starzer, which was scored for two chalumeaux or flutes, five trumpets and timpani. The dedication 'alla Regina di Moscovia' suggests the composer's St Petersburg period (1760–8) as the time of composition; not long afterwards Leopold Mozart copied out all five movements, specifying only flutes for the upper parts. He added arrangements of five numbers by Gluck (of which one is lost), and the surviving movements were subsequently attributed to Mozart *fils* as K187 (later 159c); their correct identity was revealed only in 1937.[8] However, Starzer's music did inspire Mozart's own identically scored Divertimento K188 (240b), and the whole episode offers more than a suggestion that Mozart was at least aware of the chalumeau, if only as an obsolete curiosity.

Whilst a mere half dozen chalumeaux survive, a recent listing of two-keyed

4

clarinets in various collections numbers as many as thirty-one.[9] Conversely, rather less early repertoire for the clarinet has yet come to light, nor can we yet be certain of the precise contexts in which the instrument was played. The list of music compiled by Albert Rice for *The Baroque Clarinet* (Oxford, 1992) comprises twenty-eight works by as many as thirteen composers. Despite historically significant concertos by Valentin Rathgeber (1682–1750) and a trio by one Ferdinand Kölbel, the focus of interest today remains Handel, Vivaldi and Molter, even though orchestral C and D clarinet parts have been found in the works of Caldara (1718), Conti (1719), Faber (1720), Telemann (1721, 1728) and Graupner (1754). Vivaldi's concertos RV559 and RV560 are scored for pairs of C clarinets and oboes, and besides a lively appreciation of the upper register, show a delight in exploiting the lugubrious qualities of the lower register. This difference in timbre was subsequently noted by the German author Jacob Adlung, whose *Anleitung zu der Musikalischen Gelahrtheit* (Erfurt, 1758) noted: 'The clarinet is well known. In the low register it sounds differently from the high range, and therefore one calls it chalumeau.' But no other composer before Mozart realised the distinction quite so effectively as Vivaldi. A third concerto RV556 'per la Solennità di San Lorenzo' combines aspects of the solo concerto with the concerto grosso, incorporating a large wind section with recorders, oboes, clarinets ('clareni') and bassoon.

Vivaldi's espousal of both chalumeau and clarinet is significant, since he continued to write for chalumeau even after discovering the full range of the clarinet, whose low register must have seemed less even and more veiled in sound. Documentary comparisons of the two instruments are rare, though Garsault in *Notionaire, ou mémorial raisonné* (Paris, 1761) noted the similarity of embouchure. The principal sources for playing technique relating to the two-keyed clarinet are Majer (1732) and Eisel's *Musicus Autodidaktos* (Erfurt, 1738), both of whom include fingering charts. One of Eisel's questions is 'What type of clef is used for the clarinet? One usually uses the G [treble] clef, in which case the instrument is treated in the clarino or trumpet style, yet sometimes the soprano and alto clefs are found, in which case the clarinet is handled like a chalumeau.' This nicely reflects Vivaldi's aesthetic, if not his actual practice.

A broadening of the expressive range of the two-keyed D clarinet occurs within the six concertos of Johann Melchior Molter (1696–1765) preserved in Karlsruhe.[10] A very high tessitura to g''' is employed, with notes below c'' usually treated in a purely triadic manner. Rice summarised the technical devices as wide leaps of more than one octave, triplet semiquaver figures and demisemiquaver and hemidemisemiquaver flourishes, as well as a number of grace-notes and trills.[11] But it is the slow movements (where in trumpet concertos the soloist was traditionally silent) which exhibit a cantabile and elegant *galant* style of clarinet writing which was gradually to replace the old trumpet associations. The tessitura of the Molter concertos already assumes a different design of clarinet from the early Denner specimens; indeed, there is in Nuremberg a later two-keyed clarinet by J. G. Zencker whose characteristics (including smaller mouthpiece) make it an ideal vehicle for these works. At this period we are also at the threshold of developments in mechanism; a further (third) key on some surviving clarinets extended the lower range downwards a semitone from f to e, which became the norm in Mozart's day.

The classical clarinet

After the middle of the eighteenth century the linking of clarinet and trumpet sound – the Italian term 'clarinetto' is a simple diminutive of 'clarino' – gave way to a radical redefining of the aesthetics of clarinet writing towards emulation of the human voice. This coincided with a period which by the time of Mozart's maturity established the five-keyed clarinet (though the pace and progress of this development was by no means uniform throughout Europe), and brought about changes in design which encouraged a greater flexibility throughout the compass. The improvement of response in the lowest (chalumeau) register was to prove especially significant by the time of Mozart's collaboration with Anton Stadler.

Paris

Mozart's early travels brought him to several European cities where the clarinet was gaining an important foothold. He first visited Paris for five months from November 1763. 'Clarinette: sorte de hautbois' must have been the briefest entry (as well as one of the least accurate) in the *Encyclopédie* compiled by Diderot and d'Alembert (17 volumes, Paris, 1751–65), but doubtless reflected general perceptions of the instrument at the time it appeared some ten years before Mozart's arrival. Nevertheless, important developments were already taking place. Archives of the Paris Opéra show that two German clarinettists were paid as extra players for twenty-five perform-ances of Rameau's opera *Zoroastre* (1749). Since there is no indication of clarinets in the score, their parts probably doubled those for violin or oboe, as is actually indicated in an autograph score of *Les Boréades*. However, in *Acante et Céphise* (1751) prominent clarinet parts occur in as many as thirteen sections, scored not only for clarinets in C and D (whose usage by other composers we have already observed), but for the longer, more mellow clarinets in A. Throughout the opera clarinets are usually associated with horns, whose favoured key of D contains two clearly differentiated styles: for the clarino idiom found in the Act II aria 'L'amour est heureux' D clarinets are preferred, whereas in more lyrical numbers such as the Act II *entrée* and the *entr'acte* between Acts II and III, A clarinets are used.[12]

Much of the later activity centred upon the clarinet in the 1750s involved the work of the Mannheim composer Johann Stamitz (1717–57), who worked in Paris for a year from September 1754. A number of symphonies by him with clarinets and horns were played during that decade, probably including at least one example from the collection *La Melodia Germanica* published by Venier in Paris (1758). The title page of this collection, which also contains music by Wagenseil, Kohaut and Richter, expresses a clear preference for the clarinet, stating of the symphonies that 'in place of clarinets, they may be played with two oboes, flutes or violins'.[13] Symphonies with clarinets and horns by Ruggi and by Schencker were performed in 1760 and 1761 respectively.[14]

Another important German connection with the Paris clarinet scene was the *Essai d'instruction à l'usage de ceux qui composent pour la clarinette et le cor* (Paris, 1764) by Valentin Roeser. The continuing limitations of the four-keyed clarinet outside the tonalities of its two registers is reflected in Roeser's listing of as many as seven sizes of clarinet, pitched in G, A, B♭, C, D, E and F. In Francoeur's *Diapason général* of 1772, the list extended to nine, including clarinets in B♮ and in E♭. Significantly, Roeser drew attention to the particular sound-quality of certain members of the family, such as the mellow (and rare) G clarinet. Within the *Essai* appeared a short three-movement quartet for pairs of B♭ clarinets and E♭ horns, of which Roeser writes: 'We played this piece in the presence of Mr Stamitz, during his journey to Paris . . .'.[15] The classical (if straightforward) idioms and choice of B♭ clarinets are especially significant features. The subject of individual clarinet pitches was addressed in the article on the instrument in the *Encyclopédie* supplement of 1776. The author F. D. Castilon (*fils*) makes it clear that the A clarinet was the instrument in normal usage, but that it was converted into B♭ by the employment of alternative middle joints. This is the earliest indication of the pre-eminence of today's standard pair of A and B♭ clarinets. As Eric Halfpenny has written:

The French bias in favour of the A clarinet, playing best in medium sharp keys, was perhaps influenced by the classic pitch (D basso) of the *cor de chasse*, whose association with clarinets came fairly early upon the scene in France. The horn itself, however, was a comparatively late arrival in concerted music there, so that, while in England and elsewhere crooked horns were already being played in the flat keys which best suited oboes and bassoons, the original D tonality may have remained influential for longer in France.[16]

We may note in passing that Mozart's 'Paris' Symphony K297/300a, dating from his second visit to the city in 1778, represents his introduction to the A clarinet, which he was to elevate to new heights a decade later.

The relative profile of each clarinet clearly underwent some development during the classical period, coinciding with fewer appearances of the instrument in sharp tonalities. Vandenbroeck's *Traité général* (*c.* 1795), designed for the use of composers, lends strength to the evidence for the contemporary use of clarinets pitched in four tonalities only: A, Bb, Bb and C. In confirmation of this, Lefèvre explained that the previously used seven sizes of clarinet had now been replaced with two: a C clarinet was converted by means of a *corps de rechange* to Bb, and the Bb converted into A. French preference for the C clarinet around the turn of the century was noted by Backofen in his tutor of *c.* 1803 (*Anweisung zur Klarinette*) in the course of his own advocacy of the Bb.[17] Lefèvre's tutor of 1802 (*Méthode de clarinette*) apparently confirms this (at least in relation to didactic material), since his twelve sonatas in the appendix were notated for C clarinet, with the qualification that they could be transferred to Bb clarinet by transposing the continuo down a tone. However, solo works such as those by Michel Yost testify to the established supremacy of the Bb instrument; Pleyel's concerto, published in 1797, is exceptional for its date in its scoring for C clarinet with alternative solo parts for flute or cello.

Mannheim

Mozart visited Mannheim during the winter of 1777 and again for a month the following year. The court orchestra enjoyed a reputation unrivalled in Europe, and was described by the historian Charles Burney as 'an army of generals, equally fit to plan a battle as to fight it'. Schubart was moved to observe, 'Its *forte* is like thunder, its crescendo like a great waterfall, its diminuendo the splashing of a crystalline river disappearing into the distance, its *piano* a breath of spring'. Mozart quickly became friendly with the Konzertmeister Cannabich and others, including the Kapellmeister Holzbauer and the flautist J. B. Wendling. Although he expressed an interest in remaining in Mannheim, it soon became clear that no position was to be made available for him.

Clarinets had become officially part of the court orchestra sometime after July 1759. As we have noted, the celebrated Mannheim composer Johann Stamitz had already encountered the clarinet during his stay in Paris, where he conducted the private orchestra of the wealthy patron A.-J. -J. le Riche de la Pouplinière at his palace at Passy. The Parisian writer Ancelet was so impressed by the combination of horns and clarinets (probably as a result of hearing Stamitz's works) that he stated, 'The horns please still more when they accompany clarinets, instruments unknown till now in France and which have on our hearts and on our ears rights which were unknown to us. Of what use they could be to our composers in their music!'[18] It seems likely that the Clarinet Concerto by Stamitz was written in Paris for a virtuoso who could handle its substantial technical demands. The choice of B♭ clarinet as solo instrument in such an early work is highly significant and marks the beginning of its almost universal dominance as a concerto instrument. Stamitz's Concerto was first brought to public attention in 1936 in an article by Peter Gradenwitz.[19] Its identification as a work of Johann rather than his son Carl (which has now found universal acceptance) is based on stylistic rather than documentary evidence, the Regensburg manuscript merely ascribing it 'del Sig^n Stamitz'. In support of this attribution Gradenwitz drew attention to the concerto's heroic gestures, varied repetitions of material, use of thematic development and structural discipline. The degree of solo virtuosity is in fact greater than in most later Mannheim concertos, incorporating use of the low register and some very characteristic figuration, which (unlike some contemporary concertos) make the solo part entirely idiomatic for the clarinet and quite unsuitable for any other instrument. Leaps range over more than two octaves and there is also some high writing up to e''', which resembles Molter's clarino-type writing. It is significant that the Adagio relies for its effect on florid gesture rather than the slow cantabile cultivated by later composers. The final Poco presto, whilst typically less demanding than the opening movement, incorporates wide-ranging gestures which show a real feeling for appropriate idiom.

Carl Stamitz (1745–1801) was a leading figure among the second generation of Mannheim orchestral composers, both prolific and cosmopolitan in style, a widely travelled performer and a major contributor to solo literature for the clarinet. His works include a number of quartets for clarinet with string trio, of which the earliest set of six Op. 8 was published in Paris in 1773. He cultivated extensively the genre of the *symphonie concertante*, including two works for clarinet and bassoon,[20] one work (1778) for two clarinets or clarinet and violin, and a *Concerto per 7 stromenti principali* for flute, oboe, C clarinet, two horns, violin and cello. Identification and numbering of Stamitz's solo clarinet concertos has been inconsistent, though recent scholarship lists a total of ten, of which five were originally published between 1777 and 1793.[21] All are for Bb clarinet, with the exception of a concerto in F, for which C clarinet and oboe are specified as alternatives. A number of the concertos may have been written in collaboration with the virtuoso (and composer) Joseph Beer, whose name is included on at least one title page.[22]

Carl Stamitz's concertos and their solo writing were extensively analysed by Helmut Boese in his dissertation *Die Klarinette als Soloinstrument in der Musik der Mannheimer Schule* (Dresden, 1940). He noted that the clarinet was an ideal vehicle for the Mannheim style, with its large range, potential for dynamic contrasts and virtuoso capabilities. The first movements are varied in form and content, whereas the finales adhere to a rondo pattern with dance or character titles such as allemande, menuet or à la chasse. The figuration is freely based on diatonic scales and arpeggios, within solo parts notated only in F and C. High notes are not characteristic, with an upper limit generally restricted to *d'''*, but occasionally ascending to *eb'''*, *e'''*, *f'''* and on a single occasion *g'''*. The leaps so beloved of Mozart are already in evidence, though generally encompassing little more than two octaves. The opening movement of an Eb concerto preserved in Darmstadt shows an integration of chalumeau figuration into the melodic contours, which again foreshadows Mozart in a quite striking fashion. However, it is entirely typical that low alberti figuration in the finale of the same work is accompanied by string chords, rather than supporting melodic ideas elsewhere in the texture, as became Mozart's practice. Overall, Stamitz adopts a lyricism which is uncomplicated by contrapuntal considerations and in the slow movements reveals a cantabile aspect of the clarinet which was to prove highly seductive to later composers. Despite its increasingly characterful chalumeau register, the heart of the clarinet lay within its upper register, exploited by Stamitz in an effective manner which anticipates Mozart.

A number of other composers with Mannheim associations were attracted to the clarinet. A special case is the Bohemian Franz Pokorný (1729–94), who studied with Johann Stamitz before 1745 and wrote two concertos for Bb clarinet, of which the second is dated 1765. The solo parts are marked respectively 'per il Clarinetto primo' and 'per il Clarinetto secondo', a distinction found also in Francoeur's treatise. The second work implies an important specialisation in the chalumeau register, which is highly relevant to Stadler's technique a generation later. Of younger composers, Ernst Eichner (1740–77) wrote a Concerto in E♭ which was published in Paris during his last year, whilst in addition one of his five oboe concertos (also in E♭) was transcribed for clarinet. Franz Anton Dimler (1753–1827) wrote a concerto in B♭, which was probably the work played by his clarinettist son at a Munich concert in 1795. Christian Cannabich (1731–98), director of the Mannheim orchestra from 1774, taught composition to the clarinettist Georg-Friedrich Fuchs (1752–1821), a German by birth but mainly active in Paris from 1784. A pupil also of Haydn, Fuchs composed many clarinet works, including a concerto and a *symphonie concertante* with horn. His Op. 1, a set of duos for clarinet and violin, was published the year after Mozart's death. The tradition of Mannheim virtuoso clarinet writing was continued in works by Peter von Winter, Franz Danzi, and especially the brilliant clarinet virtuoso Franz Tausch (1762–1817), whose compositions and playing won him much adulation. The lexicographer E. L. Gerber heard him in Paris at a concert in 1793: 'What versatility in gradation of tone. At one moment the low whisper of leaves borne along by the soft breath of the zephyr; at another his instrument soared above all others in a torrent of brilliant arpeggios.'[23] Fétis considered him the match of Beer and Stadler, having at the same time more charm and softness in his playing than either of them.[24] Stadler found himself unfavourably compared with Tausch in a review of a Berlin concert around the same time. In 1782 Paris also saw publication of one of the four clarinet concertos by the Bohemian Rosetti (*c.* 1750–92). Another of Stadler's fellow-countrymen to have composed clarinet concertos was Leopold Kozeluch (1747–1818), whose two concertos in E♭ were written prior to 1790. By comparison with the works of Carl Stamitz, a richer chromatic vein is an important distinguishing feature of his solo writing.

London

The arrival of the clarinet in orchestras throughout Europe has been the subject of considerable recent research.[25] Although Paris and Mannheim appear to have been the most important centres, London was already proving significant by the time of Mozart's fifteen-month visit beginning in 1764. The German Carl Weichsell, oboist at the King's Theatre, was probably the 'Mr Wrexell' who played the clarinet on 28 December 1760 in Arne's *Thomas and Sally*.[26] He may also have participated in Arne's *Artaxerxes* and J. C. Bach's *Orione*, both of 1762. The type of instrument used for these works is unknown,

11

though Rice has drawn attention to a remark in *The Harmonicon* of 1830 (pp. 57–8) by a writer known simply by the initials 'J. P.': 'I conjecture, also, that it [the clarinet] is of German invention, for I have heard that a native of that country played on a clarionet with three keys only, many years ago, in this country'. At the first performance of Bach's *Orione* on 19 February 1763 Burney was very struck 'with the new and happy use he had made of wind instruments, this being the first time that clarinets had admission in our opera orchestra'.[27] Arne links his C clarinets with horns for a hunting scene in *Thomas and Sally*, but in one of the two scenes with clarinets in *Artaxerxes* associates the instrument with the subject of love. That this was a transitional stage between old and new styles of clarinet writing is illustrated by the use of D and B♭ clarinets in Bach's *Orione*. Notwithstanding his inclusion of the rare *clarinette d'amour* in D in his opera *Temistocle,* Bach was to gravitate increasingly towards the B♭ clarinet in his orchestral and chamber music. Significantly, he is known to have been especially friendly to the young Mozart, remaining an important influence for many years afterwards. Carl Friedrich Abel's Symphony Op. 7 No. 6 in E♭, whose scoring includes a pair of B♭ clarinets, was copied out by Mozart during his London visit and for many years was ascribed to him as K18.

Many of the simple English tutors published during the late eighteenth century assume the supremacy of the C clarinet, and this may have been the instrument preferred by amateurs. For example, the *Compleat Instructions for the Clarinet* published by S. A. & P. Thompson states:

The only Keys in which Clarinet Music is printed are C and F, for which a C Clarinet must be used: But as This Instrument is often required to Play in Concert with Bassoons and other Instruments, in the Key of B♭ or E♭, it is necessary in this case to use a B [*sic*] Clarinet, which will agree with them tho' the parts for this Instrument are written and play'd a Note higher than those of the other Instruments . . .

The A clarinet seems to have been virtually unknown in England at this time.

The first British-born professional clarinettists to emerge in the history of the instrument in England were John Mahon (*c*. 1749–1834) and his brother William (*c*. 1751–1816). John Mahon made his début concerto performance in November 1772 in his home town of Oxford, and the following year appeared in London, where he later took up residence. One of the foremost performers of his day, John Mahon participated in many provincial festivals between 1773 and 1823, also playing with the orchestras of all the major London venues. The parts of his first concerto, published by Welcker *c*. 1775, have not been found; his second was published *c*.1786 by J. Bland, though the work itself pre-dates 16 February 1775, when it was performed by Mahon in a concert given by Arne at the Haymarket Theatre.[28] Although the title page states that the concerto may be played by 'Clarinett, Hoboy, German Flute or Violin', the solo part was printed already transposed for B♭ clarinet, indicating Mahon's principal choice of instrument. The solo writing is assured and virtuosic, incorporating a degree of chromaticism and a tessitura up to g'''; however, the chalumeau register is conspicuously avoided, perhaps reflecting the relative lack of development of English instruments in this area of the compass.[29]

*

In sum, therefore, Mozart's espousal of the clarinet took place during a period of intense orchestral and solo development of the instrument. Three of the most important European musical centres visited by Mozart played an important role in establishing the clarinet. By the 1770s and 1780s the B♭ clarinet was almost universally chosen for concertos, in the context of a general consensus that each pitch was also differentiated by its timbre. Outside England the chalumeau register played a significant part in solo idioms, largely in diatonic scales and arpeggios, but was not used to accompany other elements in the texture. Leaps became part of the solo vocabulary as the clarinet's potential for agility became appreciated. Tutors for the instrument give some indication of different usage, France establishing an important didactic tradition, whilst England catered for a burgeoning amateur market. Clarinet writing in concertos and chamber music belies the caution with which the clarinet was handled in the orchestra as late as Beethoven's first two symphonies. In its five-keyed configuration which by this time had become the norm, the clarinet had become fluent over a large compass, though only within certain amenable keys. More significantly, its lyrical qualities had begun to be widely cultivated. By the mid-1780s Schubart was characterising the clarinet as overflowing with love, with an indescribable sweetness of expression.

Mozart, Stadler and the clarinet

Introduction: Salzburg

Mozart's early encounters with the clarinet were somewhat fleeting. At least one writer has speculated that he may have heard the instrument as early as 1763 at an 'academy' of the Mannheim orchestra in Schwetzingen.[1] As we have noted, he certainly encountered the clarinet during his London visit of 1764, and he first employed the instrument in his own music in the Divertimento K113, written in November 1771 for the private orchestra of a patron in Milan. Generations of scholars have repeated Otto Jahn's assertion that there were no clarinets in Salzburg, but this has recently been called into question by Kurt Birsak.[2] His research uncovered a mention of the clarinet in Salzburg in an *Aufsatz und Specification deren Spielleithen nothbetärftigen Instrumenten in französischem Thon* (*Essay and Specifications of the Instruments in the French Pitch required by Military Bandsmen*), dated 1769. Within this document is the entry '2 clarinets in D with mouthpiece and long B key as well as a joint for tuning it into C'.[3] In the requests for new instruments, the argument was put forward that, after years of use, they had become 'gradually unfit for use', so they must have been employed for some considerable time already. Birsak draws attention to the fact that the public performances of the military bands were still at that time exclusively the duty of the nine professional musicians who formed a band of *Musikalischen Parade Instrumente* of oboes, horns and bassoons. A semi-official section of the band comprised the 'Turkish Music', which apart from percussion was made up of two clarinets, two trumpets in Eb tuneable also to D or Db, and four fifes; by 1803 it had achieved equal status with the parade band. Another early mention of clarinets is in a general inventory of the fortress from 1776, according to which the Company of Grenadiers owned two 'clarinets with straps and cases'.[4]

There survives in Salzburg a three-keyed D clarinet which corresponds remarkably well with the 1769 description and is indeed at very low French pitch.[5] An even older one with two keys by the same maker may well be its predecessor in the band. Repertoire by Michael Haydn for this type of instrument includes a thirty-six-bar soprano aria, 'Kommt her ihr Menschen' (1772), with C clarinet obbligato in clarino style within the range $g'-d'''$. Additionally, one of twelve minuets by Haydn dating from 1774 has inserted into the horn parts the instruction 'Clarinet in G'; since the piece is in A major this leaves some doubt as to precisely which clarinet is intended.[6] In further sets of minuets of 1786 and 1794 clarinet parts are simple and were arranged so that they could be played by a flautist or oboist alternately. A quintet of 1790 is more demanding, apparently requiring a specialist player of a classical, five-keyed clarinet.[7] Clarinets were introduced into the Salzburg court orchestra only in 1804/5.[8]

On balance, it seems likely that the old-fashioned clarino role of the clarinet would not have attracted the special attention of the young Mozart, who encountered abroad an instrument with quite different tonal capabilities. But rather confusingly, the earliest surviving clarinet music by Michael Haydn incorporates idioms which are remarkably advanced. A large-scale nine-movement divertimento completed on 4 August 1764 has two *concertante* movements for A clarinet, which surpass virtually all contemporary works in their technical demands.[9] The solo movements are an Andante in 3/4 time and a *Spirituoso* in 4/4, in which the clarinet part ranges from the lowest written note e to d''' and contains many leaps of one-and-a-half octaves. Chromaticism is confined to the upper register, but assigns prominence to notes which make it virtually certain that a five-keyed clarinet was intended. The chalumeau register is neither emphasised nor neglected. Birsak assumed that a touring virtuoso passing through Salzburg would by now have been identified, and that Haydn was simply completing a work started earlier in his career, though the date does seem to indicate a Salzburg *Finalmusik*. In any event, this rare and early usage of the classical clarinet in Mozart's home city is of considerable historical interest. Furthermore, to the student of Mozart's Clarinet Concerto Haydn's espousal of the A clarinet lends to this divertimento a special further significance. The earliest known concertos for A clarinet were written only during the 1780s by Theodor von Schacht (1748–1823) of the Regensburg court.

Mozart and the clarinet before 1780

During 1764 Mozart must have become aware of the singing qualities of the clarinet and of the sensuous quality of clarinet thirds which are a conspicuous element in the Abel symphony he copied out. His own three-movement Divertimento K113 (for clarinets, horns and strings) develops Abel's lyrical clarinet idioms to incorporate a degree of chromaticism. A separate surviving wind score for K113 introduces pairs of oboes, cors anglais and bassoons. The question of whether these parts were intended to substitute for the original winds in a later performance at Salzburg when clarinets were not available (as seems likely), or whether the second version comprises a cumulative ten-part wind scoring, has proved controversial.[10] The title page of the five-movement Divertimento in E♭ K166/159d for full ten-part wind ensemble without strings indicates its provenance as Salzburg (24 March 1773), which has only added to the confusion. However, the classical nature of the B♭ clarinet writing in this work and its companion K186/159b scarcely argues for Mozart's temporary access to the Salzburg *Feldeninstrumenten*, but rather suggests a forthcoming commitment with an ensemble in Milan, as traditionally assumed.[11]

As we noted in Chapter 1, by the time of Mozart's arrival in Mannheim in 1777 the vibrant tradition of clarinet writing had already explored the instrument's potential to a greater extent than elsewhere. Mozart thought Cannabich the best conductor he had encountered and during his return visit the following year wrote to his father on 3 December 1778: 'Ah, if only we had clarinets too! You cannot imagine the glorious effect of a symphony with flutes, oboes and clarinets.'[12] The orchestral clarinet players admired by Mozart on that occasion were probably Fuchs, Franz Tausch and his father Jacob. An important exchange of letters took place during 1778, when Mozart was in Paris, his father writing on 29 June:

Mme Dusek has sent me a letter of introduction to a certain virtuoso on the clarinet, M. Joseph Beer, who is in the service of the Prince de Lambsec, Chief Equerry to the King of France. Tell me whether I am to send it to you. Try to see M. Beer.

Mozart's reply on 9 July was revealing:

As for the letter of recommendation to Herr Beer, I don't think it is necessary to send it to me: so far I have not made his acquaintance; I only know that he is a dissolute sort of fellow. I really do not like to associate with such people, as it does one no credit; and, frankly, I should not like to give him a letter of recommendation – indeed, I should feel positively ashamed to do so – even if he could do something for me! But, as it is, he is by no means respected here – and a great many people do not know him at all.[13]

As Pamela Weston has pointed out, Beer had an international reputation unequalled by Anton Stadler; he was about to launch upon an extensive European tour, and could probably have benefited Mozart considerably.[14]

Mozart's 'Paris' Symphony K297/300a is notable for its large orchestration rather than for the prominence of its A clarinet parts. The oboe concerto sketch K293/416f in F has clarinets in C, as part of an orchestral palette within

16

an amenable key for the soloist. Their very presence in such a work represents an important stage in Mozart's appreciation of the clarinet. His final involvement with the instrument before meeting Stadler in Vienna may be observed in *Idomeneo*, written for the Munich court (which was now home of the former Mannheim orchestra) and first performed on 29 January 1781. The scoring includes clarinets in A, B♭, B and C, revealing an astute awareness of appropriate dramatic contexts in which to use the instrument.[15] Idiomatic use of clarinets in (major and minor) thirds and sixths down to c' nevertheless excludes the chalumeau register below the note b.

Anton Stadler

Anton Stadler's life and career has been the subject of research by a number of scholars, including Martha Kingdon-Ward, Karl Maria Pisarowitz, Pamela Weston and Pamela Poulin.[16] Pisarowitz discovered records showing Stadler's birthplace as Bruck an der Leitha, outside Vienna; three years after his birth in 1753 the family moved to Vienna, where his brother Johann was born. Though contemporary dictionaries report that both brothers played the clarinet and basset horn, the *Journal des Luxus un der Moden* of 1801 described Anton as 'a great artist on many wind instruments',[17] whilst in a letter dated 6 November 1781 to Ignatz von Beecke of the orchestra at Wallerstein, Anton writes that he and his brother 'can also play a little violin and viol [*sic*]'.[18]

A programme for a concert on 21 March 1773 at the Kärtnertortheater bears witness to the start of the Stadlers' career in Vienna. They again featured in a concert on 19 December 1775. On 12 and 14 March 1780 they took part in a concerto for five winds by Joseph Starzer. Some important contemporary events have been charted by Pamela Poulin:

Until 1782 Anton and Johann held various positions. According to the open account books of the imperial court of 1779 they were hired by the court on a per-service basis. A concert programme of 12 March identifies the brothers as being in the service of Count Carl of Palm. As of October 1780 Anton was employed by the Piaristen religious order of Maria Treu as a 'manorial musician'. In 1781 Anton was in the service of Count Dimitri Galizin. In the same year Kaiser Joseph II designated their services as 'indispensable'.[19]

Then came the unsuccessful application for work at Wallerstein, in which it was claimed that they could supplement orchestral skills with duets, concertos, wind octets and basset horn trios with a colleague named Griesbacher. Mozart's first encounter with Stadler may have been around this time, following his own move to Vienna. In October 1781 he wrote of the first performance of the sextet version of his E♭ Serenade K375: 'The six gentlemen who executed it are poor beggars who, however, play quite well together, particularly the first clarinet and the two horns'. On 8 February 1782 the Stadlers were invited to join the orchestra of the Viennese imperial court, and the following year they were members of the emperor's *Harmonie,* in which Stadler played second clarinet.[20] Stadler's evident preoccupation with the chalumeau register is significant in view of Mozart's subsequent exploitation of its idiomatic potential.[21]

The earliest documented evidence of Mozart's connection with Stadler dates from a year or two later. The clarinettist's playing evoked the following response in Johann Friedrich Schink's *Litterarische Fragmente*:

'My thanks to you, brave virtuoso! I have never heard the like of what you contrived with your instrument. Never should I have thought that a clarinet could be capable of imitating the human voice as it was imitated by you. Indeed, your instrument has so soft and lovely a tone that no one with a heart can resist it – and I have one, dear Virtuoso; let me thank you. I heard music for wind instruments today, too, by Herr Mozart, in four movements, viz. four horns, two oboes, two bassoons, two clarinets, two basset horns, a double bass, and at each instrument sat a master – oh, what a glorious effect it made – glorious and grand, excellent and sublime! (p. 286)

Schink here clearly refers to a performance of Mozart's Serenade for thirteen instruments K361/370a, which probably formed part of Stadler's benefit concert at the National Court Theatre advertised in the *Wienerblättchen* of 23 March 1784: 'Herr Stadler senior, in present service of His Majesty the Emperor, will hold a musical concert for his own benefit, at which will be given, among other well chosen pieces, a great wind piece of a very special kind composed by Herr Mozart'. The Serenade K361/370a was formerly thought to have been written for the Munich court in 1780 or 1781, though for a variety of reasons 1783–4 has now been accepted as a far more likely period for its composition.[22] As well as the exploration of idiomatic and progressive basset horn writing exhibited in the Serenade, its clarinet parts show an enormous increase in understanding of the instrument. Barely more than a week after this first documented performance came the première of Mozart's Piano Quintet K452 on 1 April, which included parts for both composer and clarinettist.

Although the eloquence of Mozart's clarinet writing for Stadler testifies to a remarkable musical relationship, surviving evidence of their personal friendship remains fragmentary. But Mozart's nickname for the clarinettist reveals a shared sense of humour; 'Notschibinitschibi' is a combination of two words – 'Notschibi' meaning a poor booby or miser and 'Nitschibi' a young man of follies.[23]

The basset horn and Masonic associations

Mozart developed a love affair with the basset horn during the 1780s which must be understood before the special fruits of his friendship with Stadler can be properly appreciated. Recent performances on early basset horns or copies have helped to illuminate Mozart's fascination for the instrument, since its extraordinary acoustical make-up produces a tone-quality which can truly be described as other-worldly; this derives from the retention of a bore which is scarcely wider than on the clarinet, a much shorter instrument. The basset horn came to be associated with Masonic ritual, for which its special character was ideally suited. Mozart joined the small lodge 'Zur Wohlthätigkeit' ('Benificence') on 14 December 1784, whilst Anton Stadler was admitted to the 'Zum Palmbaum' ('Palm Tree') lodge on 27 September the following year. In December 1785 the Emperor Joseph II decreed that the number of Viennese lodges be reduced from eight to two, Mozart's being fused into the new lodge 'Zur neugekrönten Hoffnung' ('New Crowned Hope') in 1786.

The arrival in Vienna of the Bohemian players Anton David and Vincent Springer proved an important catalyst for Mozart's basset horn writing. They had already generated considerable publicity as early as 1782, when their performance at Ludwiglust 'on largely unknown instruments which they call basset horns' was cited by C. F. Cramer the following year.[24] Mozart's espousal of the basset horn really began in earnest in late 1783 when he produced over a period of two years thirteen works for that instrument. These are K436, 437, 438, 439, 346/439a, 439b, 452a, 477/479a, 411/484a, 484b, 484c, 410/484d and 484e, the last of which dates from the end of 1785. This remarkable activity was undoubtedly brought about by the availability of four excellent clarinet and basset horn players – the Stadlers, David and Springer – who in combination must have inspired the scoring of Mozart's Serenade K361/370a, in addition to more ritualistic works such as the Adagio K411/484a. Around this time the two visitors won further fulsome praise from J. N. Forkel in his *Musikalischer Almanach* for the year 1784, published in Leipzig; Forkel added that the instrument was still unknown and was said to be a kind of bass clarinet.[25]

David and Springer had come to Vienna in an attempt to find permanent employment, but were not successful, for on 20 October 1785 the Palm Tree and Three Eagles lodges of the Viennese Masonic order sponsored a concert to raise funds for their journey home. Mozart and Stadler performed at this concert. Mozart's most important piece of Masonic music originated in the deaths of two brothers: Georg August, Duke of Mecklenburg-Strelitz, and Franz, Count Esterházy of Galántha. On 17 November was held a Lodge of Sorrows for which Mozart used an extraordinary and fortuitous collection of musicians in his *Maurerische Trauermusik* K477/479a. The clarinet part was probably intended for Stadler and the contrabassoon part for Theodor Lotz. The initial scoring also included a single basset horn, but two more were added by Mozart, presumably to allow the participation of David and Springer. Robbins Landon has noted the heavy symbolism and the work's illustration of Mozart's total involvement with the theories and philosophies of death.[26] Mozart appeared again at another benefit concert for the Bohemian pair at the Crowned Hope Lodge on 15 December 1785, for which the items included 'A Parthie [suite] composed by Brother Stadler for six wind instruments, for which the Hon. Brother Locz [*sic*] will play the great octave bassoon'. Stadler's Partita is no longer extant.[27] Significantly, Mozart wrote nothing further for the basset horn after this concert until 1788 (K537b and 549).

The early history of the basset horn was one of rapid development. The first types, with sickle shape tube modelled on the oboe da caccia, borrowed the box or *Buch* just above its bell from instruments such as the rackett to achieve an extension down from written *e* to the tonic *c*. Neither the simplest instruments with four to six keys (probably *c.* 1760 and equivalent in development to the three-keyed clarinet) nor some seven-keyed basset horns by the supposed inventors A. and M. Mayrhofer are furnished with any intervening notes.[28] A six-keyed basset horn of this design is described by J. G. L. von Wilke in his *Musikalisches Handwörtenbuch* (Weimar, 1786) and a seven-keyed version by E. L. Gerber in his *Historisch-biographisches Lexicon der Tonkünstler* (1790–2). A considerable attempt to clarify the complexities of basset horn history has been made by Nicholas Shackleton in his article 'The earliest basset horns', in the *Galpin Society Journal*, 40 (1987).

Having become established in the 1780s, the more readily constructed shape of two limbs joined at an angle by a knee is described in the *Musikalisches Lexicon* (1802) by H. C. Koch.[29] This design is widely illustrated in organological literature, for example by Baines in *Woodwind Instruments and their History*. Surviving specimens testify to the provision of a key for *d* at this time, even though as late as 1810–11 the somewhat conservative *Vollständige theoretisch-praktische Musikschule* by Joseph Fröhlich remarked that this note was not always present. Its addition probably constitutes the improvement of 1782 attributed by C. F. Cramer to Theodor Lotz.[30] This Pressburg

(Bratislava) maker was to become a seminal figure in the musical relationship of Mozart and Stadler (see pp. 20, 25ff). Eight-keyed basset horns of this type were constructed in the 1780s and continued to be described much later, for example as late as 1840 in G. Schilling's *Universal-Lexicon der Tonkunst*. In addition to the basset horns in G and in F used by Mozart, they were also constructed in E, E♭ and D, according to J. G. Albrechtsberger's *Gründliche Anweisung zur Composition* (Leipzig, 1790).

Early in 1796 Schönfeld described the Stadlers as 'accomplished artists both on the ordinary clarinet and also on the basset clarinet, on which difficult instrument they have perfected control of tone-production, nuance, expression and facility'.[31] It has been convincingly claimed that this is a reference to the basset horn, whose relatively narrower bore made it especially difficult to play. Similar terminology was used by Gottfried Weber in 1822,[32] and recurs in still later sources. The attribution to the Stadlers of the addition to the basset horn of low *c♯* and *d♯* has some definite basis, even though the vast majority of surviving instruments of the period have only *c* and *d* keys, including examples by Lotz. Albrechtsberger mentions an exceptional basset horn with chromatic extension (*d♯*, *d*, *c♯*, *c*) and four-octave range developed by the Stadler brothers of Vienna. Whether or not both chromatic notes became available at once, Mozart's attitude to the improvement at first shows restraint; the second basset horn part of the Serenade K361/370a has but a single passage in the Trio I of the first Minuet requiring *d* and *e♭*, whilst there is a single low c in the first movement. If the basset horns normally used by David and Springer were seven-keyed instruments pitched in G, as Cramer suggests, both players must have been newly equipped for the Serenade, perhaps with basset horns in F belonging to the Stadlers. Shackleton has observed that on the eighteenth-century design of a flat *Buch* even the provision of *d* is not accomplished without difficulty because the hole to be covered is far off the line of the lever controlling it. It is just possible to add a close-standing key to provide low *e♭*, of which there are later examples on instruments of this design probably dating from 1800–20.[33] Though unknown on any basset horn of this design, *c♯* must also have been available to Stadler, as witnessed by Albrechtsberger's remarks; indeed, the note is required in the lowest basset horn part of Mozart's *Notturno* K436. It is perhaps significant that Stadler's own *Terzetti* provide an *ossia* an octave higher whenever the note occurs in his lowest basset horn part.

Shackleton makes the important point that although instruments made for Stadler by Lotz must have been furnished with a flat *Buch*, other makers were making basset horns of various other designs well before the end of the eighteenth century, in which the three bores in the box were in a triangle rather than beside each other in a flat box. Such makers include Grundmann and August Grenser in Dresden, Doleisch in Prague and Kirst in Potsdam. It is significant that Doleisch added an *eb* mechanism before 1800, an easier operation where the box was triangular.[34] The relative reputation of Lotz has thus perhaps been enhanced by Cramer's reference and by his association with Mozart and Stadler, though he was undoubtedly one of the seminal figures in the basset horn's development. We may note in conclusion that the earliest known basset horns to incorporate *c#* (in a triangular *Buch*) were made by Heinrich Grenser (and later by Grenser and Wiesner) and now form part of collections in Zurich, Basel, Ann Arbor and Boston. These instruments, however, date from twenty years or so after Mozart's death.

Mozart's clarinet writing, 1781–7

The beginning of Mozart's Vienna period immediately witnessed a progression of idiom within his clarinet writing. The first (sextet) version of the Serenade K375 represents an important development of the cantabile qualities of the upper register and the characteristic richness of paired thirds. The chalumeau register – the lowest part of the clarinet's compass ranging from *e* to *f'* – gradually achieved the status of a melodic resource in its own right, though in both the sextet and octet versions of K375 the second clarinet alberti figuration is as yet situated relatively high and also makes use of the 'throat notes' *g'* –*bb'*, immediately below the clarinet's principal upper register. The Andante of the C minor Serenade K388/384a represents an expansion of idiom, since some of the oscillating accompanying sixths now encompass the true chalumeau register. Mozart's clarinet writing for the theatre at this period illustrates a similar development of idiom. For example, Belmonte's aria 'Ich baue ganz auf deine Stärke' in *Die Entführung aus dem Serail* introduces accompanying triplets in the second clarinet, although these are as yet built on arpeggios rising from *c'* and *b* rather than from the chalumeau register itself. This opera also contains parts for basset horns in the aria 'Traurigkeit', incorporating some prominent accompaniment, though not within the chalumeau register.[35]

The Serenade K361/370a brings together an ever-increasing appreciation of the vocal qualities of the clarinet and basset horn, and these remain of paramount importance throughout the work. At the same time, exploration of possibilities in the chalumeau register enters a new phase, especially within the Variations. Indeed, the Serenade represents the single most important milestone in Mozart's development as a composer for the clarinet and basset horn. The sheer range of its textures remains unsurpassed, and lays the foundation for his subsequent solo music for these instruments. Of smaller-scale works from this period the Adagio K411/484a for two clarinets and three basset horns exhibits a remarkable emotional intensity which is also a feature of the diminutive Adagio K410/484d for two basset horns and bassoon. Masonic music of this period produced some unusual scorings, such as the inclusion of a single clarinet with oboes, horns and strings in the cantata *Die Maurerfreude* K471. The twenty-five movements for three basset horns which constitute K439b illustrate a mastery of the medium which already begins to make comprehensible the achievement of the Clarinet Concerto half a dozen years later. Chromaticism in the upper register is handled freely, and there is effective (though more diatonic) use of the very bottom of the range.

The closely related Notturni K346/439a, 436, 439 and the later K549 combine three voices with the basset horns, whilst K438 prefers an accompaniment of two B♭ clarinets and basset horn in F. Most extended is 'Mi lagnerò tacendo' K437 in the key of G, scored for two A clarinets and basset horn in G. This is a highly unusual combination of colours, and Mozart elsewhere avoids this tonality in writing for clarinets. All his other chamber music prior to the Quintet K581 was conceived for B♭ rather than A clarinet. The basset horn in G played a crucial role in the gestation of the Clarinet Concerto, though K437 is the only complete piece by Mozart to include it. The significance of this Notturno within the history of Mozart's clarinet music will only become clear when a true chronology of his clarinet and basset horn pieces of 1783–5 can be established.

The Clarinet Trio K498 was written for the pianist Francesca von Jacquin and must have been first played at the family house, with the participation of Stadler and Mozart himself. It undoubtedly reflects the favourite techniques and idioms of each of the players; in Stadler's case these included accompaniment figuration now firmly within the chalumeau range, as well as melodic figures including that part of the compass. In the theatre *Don Giovanni* (1787) makes increasing use of the clarinet throughout the two acts, notably within some telling chalumeau accompaniment to the trio of voices near the end of the finale to Act I. It is in this opera rather than *Le nozze di Figaro* (1786) that clarinets begin to threaten the predominance of the oboes as the principal woodwind colouring. There is some justification for the recent assertion that at the end of the eighteenth century the relatively new clarinet came to symbolise progress and new ideals, whereas the oboe retained an association with the aristocracy and the monarchy.[36]

Three piano concertos from 1785–6 (K482 in E♭, K488 in A and K491 in C minor) mark the transference to the orchestra of the clarinet idioms absorbed during the period 1783–5, and show an abundance of serenade influence. Most significant in the light of later developments is the emergence of the A clarinet in K488, and Mozart's establishment elsewhere of a special character for this tonality, for example in the terzetto 'Ah taci, ingiusto core!' in Act II of *Don Giovanni*. The A major Piano Concerto K488 is the most distant in mood from the serenades and divertimenti, since this tonality was never cultivated in works for *Harmonie* octet or for an ensemble with basset horns. The clarinets contribute to its luxuriant texture largely within their upper register, though with some chalumeau accompaniment in the second clarinet part of the Adagio.[37]

Mozart's pupil Attwood noted (*NMA, Attwood-Studien*, pp. 156–7) that 'The Clarinette must always be written in C or in F', and this principle lies at the heart of Mozart's own clarinet writing, notwithstanding exceptions such as the A clarinet parts in the D minor Kyrie K341/368a. An annotation in Attwood's hand adds that 'the Clarinett is very usefull instead of the oboes when the Key has a number of Flats or Sharps'. In Mozart's case the choice of tonality and instrumentation must have been more intertwined than this might imply, though the view of clarinets and oboes as alternatives is supported by many of his symphonic and dramatic contexts. During a handful of years between 1781 and 1787 Mozart had assimilated a huge variety of technical and aesthetic possibilities for the clarinet; the wide range of idioms represented by the music of 1783–5 had found its way into both the concert room and the theatre. In particular, the A clarinet had already begun to mean a great deal more to him than simply an orchestral *corps de rechange*.

3

The genesis and reception of the Concerto

The newly invented clarinet

A surviving programme for a concert on 20 February 1788 documents an important milestone in the history of Mozart and Stadler, heralding the arrival of the newly extended clarinet. It announces a concert at the Hoftheater at which 'Herr Stadler the elder, in the service of his majesty the Kaiser, will play a concerto on the *Bass-Klarinet* and a variation on the *Bass-Klarinet*, an instrument of new invention and manufacture of the court instrument maker Theodor Loz [*sic*]; this instrument has two more tones than the normal clarinet'. In the same concert were given a symphony by Hayden [*sic*] and the first performance of J. F. Reichardt's *Ariadne auf Naxos*. Stadler's instrument has become known in recent times as the basset clarinet, a term coined by Jiří Kratochvíl to reflect its kinship with the basset horn. This labelling avoids confusion with the bass clarinet, whose orchestral career developed only during the nineteenth century. It seems reasonable to assume that the special clarinet referred to in 1788 had a diatonic extension of *c* and *d*, by analogy with the basset horn in normal use. It was probably pitched in B♭. Backofen's tutor (*c*. 1803) shows awareness of such an instrument: 'Another more recent and excellent invention is this, that clarinets with *d* and *c* are now being made in Vienna; this greatly improves the clarinet, because in addition to the great advantage which low *c* brings, which until now it missed so much in its favourite key of C, it now has three complete octaves, in which every clarinettist can play easily'.[1] As for the variations advertised in Stadler's 1788 programme, a number of works for clarinet by Stadler have so far been identified, including *Variations on different favourite themes* and ten variations on *You must not take amiss with me* (see Appendix 3). A possible candidate for the other clarinet work might be another of Stadler's compositions, or perhaps a B♭ Concerto whose surviving solo part in the Vienna National Library (MS 5856) has interpolated cadenzas in a different, unidentified (?Stadler's) hand, including the notes *c* and *d*. The work is listed in Supplement XV (1782–4) of the Breitkopf Catalogue, with the ascription Michel. Though this was the name used by the Parisian virtuoso Michel Yost, it seems more likely on stylistic grounds that this concerto is the work of the German Joseph Michl.[2] These cadenzas have been reproduced in two recent articles relating to Stadler.[3]

The Lotz basset clarinet must be associated with Mozart's Quintet fragment in Bb K516c, ninety-three bars of a movement which in 1828 Georg von Nissen believed to have been originally complete.[4] Basset notes occur only from bar 55, *d* then occurring seven times, occasioning notation in the bass clef an octave below pitch, as in Mozart's basset horn writing.[5] His avoidance of the tonic *c* has led some writers to assume that *d* and *eb* were the extra notes on Lotz's instrument, but the obvious parallel with the basset horn makes *c* and *d* much more likely. In fact, Mozart's initial reserve in using the extended compass of the basset clarinet resembles his earlier approach in the Serenade K361/370a, where he uses the newly available basset horn note *eb* (and even the tonic *c*) with great economy. Robert Levin reconstructed the movement and believes that the missing portion of K516c must have contained several examples of low *c*.[6] The second clarinet part to Ferrando's aria 'Ah lo veggio' from *Così fan tutte* also descends to *d* on a total of seven occasions.

In his edition of Köchel, Alfred Einstein assigned the Quintet K516c to the year 1787 on the basis of a related eight-bar Andante Rondo fragment, the neighbouring sketches of which are known to date from that year. It has further been noted that an autograph score of the G minor String Quintet K516 (1787) has its opening staves originally prepared by Mozart for a clarinet quintet ('Clarinetto in B'), and that the clefs and staves were amended by him.[7] On the other hand, Alan Tyson has claimed through the study of paper types and watermarks that K516c dates from 1790 or 1791.[8] That Mozart should have turned to a simpler *concertante* style of writing (for an instrument apparently with two rather than four extra notes) after completing the A major Quintet K581 in 1789 seems unlikely on musical grounds, however. The diatonically extended Bb basset clarinet is also the vehicle for the virtuoso obbligato to the aria 'Parto, parto' in *La clemenza di Tito*, written in the autumn of 1791 immediately before the Clarinet Concerto. There is a little evidence to suggest that it remained an important instrument during Stadler's career after Mozart's death. Among works accompanied by Stadler on a clarinet with modifications of his own invention was Soffia's aria 'Una voce al cor mi parla' from Act II of *Sargino* (1803) by Ferdinando Paer.[9] A valuable clue as to Stadler's provision of repertoire for his new instrument is the Latin parody 'Cor sincerum amore' after Mozart's aria 'Non temer, amato bene' K505, in which the obbligato piano part is transcribed for basset clarinet.[10] Poulin illustrates some contexts from Stadler's own solos and duets whose contours may have been altered from an original version for basset clarinet.[11] Of other works in which he participated, Süssmayr's cantata *Der Retter in Gefahr* presents similar evidence.

The basset clarinet in A: Mozart's Clarinet Quintet

A fully chromatic basset clarinet is mentioned for the first time in the Berlin *Musikalische Korrespondenz* of 1790, which stated that Stadler had ' . . . improved his instrument and added notes at the bottom, so that *e* is no longer the lowest note, but rather the *c* below this. He also takes the intervening the *c#* and *d#* with amazing ease.'[12] The article on the clarinettist in Gerber's *Lexicon* of 1792 confirms this evidence: ' . . . the elder Stadler . . . has, according to recent reports from Vienna from the year 1790, lengthened his instrument a third in the low register, so that instead of having *e* as the bottom note, he can play easily down to *d#*, *d*, *c#* and *c*'. Lotz died in 1792 and credit for the new instrument was henceforth claimed by Stadler, though there is no corroborative evidence that he was himself an instrument maker. By the time of Koch's *Musikalisches Lexicon* of 1802, the invention was categorically ascribed to Stadler in the year 1790. The evidence as a whole merely points to November 1790 as the date *by which* the fully chromatic basset clarinet was operational.

Mozart's Clarinet Quintet in A K581 was completed on 29 September 1789 and premièred by Stadler on 22 December of the same year at a concert given by the Tonkünstler-Societät at the Hoftheater for the benefit of widows and orphans. Also on the programme was Vincenzo Righini's cantata *Das Geburtsfest des Apoll*, which was repeated the following evening, on that occasion with Devienne's Concertino for flute, clarinet and bassoon. The soloists were Stadler and two colleagues from the National Court Orchestra. There was a further performance of the Quintet on 9 April 1790 at Count Hadik's, which is referred to in a letter written the previous day from Mozart to Michael Puchberg.[13]

The autograph scores of both the Quintet K581 and the Clarinet Concerto K622 are lost. That these were in Stadler's possession in the 1790s (together with the trios K439b) is indicated in a letter of 31 May 1800 written by Mozart's widow Constanze to his publisher André:

For information about other works of this kind you should apply to the elder Stadler, the clarinettist, who used to possess the original manuscripts of several, and has copies of some trios for basset horn that are still unknown. Stadler declares that while he was in Germany his portmanteau was stolen, with these pieces in it. Others, however, assure me that the said portmanteau was pawned there for 73 ducats; but there were, I believe, instruments and other things in it as well.[14]

The Clarinet Quintet was first published in 1802 by André in Offenbach and by Artaria in Vienna. These editions for normal A clarinet were followed when the text was prepared for the *Neue Mozart-Ausgabe* in 1958, even though its preface acknowledges earlier research establishing the basset clarinet as the intended instrument. Ten years earlier, in an article primarily relating to the Clarinet Concerto, George Dazeley instanced a number of contexts in which he surmised that the text had been altered. These were bars 41, 99–110, 114, 185, 187 and 196–7 in the first movement; bar 81 (and 116) in the Menuetto; and in the finale bars 3, 7, 13, 14 in variation I, 8 and 16 in variation II, 8 and 16 in variation III, and 1, 3, 13 and 16 in variation IV; and bar 36 of the coda.[15] Since Dazeley's article appeared, there have been further suggestions for the text's reconstruction.[16] Contemporary Artaria editions for alternative forces (for instance, with a second viola replacing the clarinet) offer some corroborative evidence. Although the melodic lines of the outer movements are greatly enhanced by restoration of the basset notes, Mozart's overall restraint in using them remains evident in the Quintet as a whole. No necessity for reconstruction is apparent in the Larghetto and scarcely any in the Menuetto. The question remains whether a fully chromatic basset extension had been developed by the time the Quintet was written. Dazeley's reconstruction implies the certain availability of c, d and also $e\flat$. A plausible restoration of the first-movement development introduces the only occurrence of $c\sharp$, thus raising doubt as to whether the note was at this stage unavailable or whether (as seems possible) Mozart was simply cautious about incorporating it into his melodic lines.

In creating the medium of the clarinet quintet, Mozart progressed significantly beyond the *concertante* style which had characterised the Oboe Quartet K370/368b and the Flute Quartets K285, 285a, 285b and 298. The clarinet part integrates with the strings and yet has many virtuoso elements which effectively introduce the range of idioms cultivated by Stadler. Especially significant is the exploitation of cantabile in the Larghetto, incorporating melodic use of the chalumeau register, which implies an assured tonal warmth. The very lowest notes are treated not in scale but in arpeggio patterns, taking account of the technical implications of the production of the basset notes by means of a single digit – the right-hand thumb. Mozart's vocal style of writing incorporates wide leaps which no singer could ever produce, exploring the clarinet as both soprano and baritone voice. Furthermore, the clarinet from time to time is assigned both descant and accompaniment to thematic material.

The eighty-nine-bar Rondo fragment K581a matches the Quintet's instrumentation and tonality and has generally been regarded as an abandoned draft of its finale. Its principal theme was eventually used in Ferrando's aria from *Così fan tutte* already mentioned. A comparison of the quintet fragment and the aria formed the basis of an article by Roland Tenschert.[17] A subsidiary violin idea at bars 41, 43 and 45 of the fragment anticipates an important idea at bars 19 and 26 of the first movement of K581, suggesting that it pre-dates the whole Quintet and not merely the finale. An arbitrary and unnecessary use of soprano, alto, tenor and bass clefs in the fragment's clarinet part within a space of fifteen bars was interpreted by Tenschert as a joke at the expense of Stadler, probably inspired by the newly invented clarinet.[18] It is during this passage that a solitary basset note $e\flat$ occurs. On account of the clef changes Poulin, following Tyson, remarks: 'It is unlikely that K581a was considered as a serious work (or as a draft for the Clarinet Quintet K581 . . .)', and she proposes a possible dating of 1790, *after* the completed Quintet.[19] However, an analogous sense of humour is displayed elsewhere by Mozart, notably in autographs written for the horn player Joseph Leutgeb.

The clarinet in A major

Although scholars and clarinettists have tended to concentrate their interest upon the design of Stadler's basset clarinet, Mozart's choice of tonality for the Quintet and the Concerto has generally escaped detailed study. We have seen that Rameau made idiomatic use of both D and A clarinets (according to context) when writing operatic numbers in D major. Francoeur's *Diapason général* (Paris, 1772) identified the particular tonal qualities of each of the nine clarinets he listed: the large G clarinet was the sweetest, saddest and most lugubrious, whilst the highest E and F clarinets were suitable only for storms and battle. Among the more common middle sizes, Francoeur clearly distinguished clarinets in A and B♭. The A had a very sweet sound, much less sombre than the G and with a greater range; it was suitable for tender, graceful melodies. On the other hand, the B♭ had a stronger sound, which could project and was therefore suitable for the grand gestures found in symphonies and overtures. The tone-quality of A and B♭ clarinets was characterised in this way by many other writers during and after Mozart's lifetime; the A was always reckoned more gentle and melancholy, sometimes even rather dull in tone. A celebrated appraisal in 1812 by a panel of judges at the Paris Conservatoire differentiated the sound of A, B♭ and C clarinets. A desire to retain all three was the reason for the decision to reject a new, supposedly omnitonic, B♭ instrument by the clarinettist-inventor Iwan Müller. The A was described as a pastoral instrument, the B♭ expressive and majestic. The latter retained its supremacy throughout the nineteenth century; Mozart's espousal of the A clarinet as a solo instrument was followed by few later composers.[20]

During the eighteenth century the perception of different key characteristics was hotly debated.[21] One popular theory was the psychological association of ever-increasing strength and brightness (or, conversely, weakness and sombreness) with the number of sharps or flats. This was a matter for controversy as early as 1713 when Mattheson's *Das neu-eröffnete Orchestre* (pp. 232–3) censured 'those people who believe that a piece in flats absolutely must sound soft and tender, while a piece in sharps must be hard, lively and joyful'. But for many commentators the function of the sharp to raise a note and of the flat to lower a note also reaffirmed these associations. For example, Rameau in 1754 wrote: ' . . . One cites the sharp as a sign of strength and joy, [as] when one raises the voice in the same cases – in anger, etc., and . . . one cites the flat as a sign of softness and weakness, etc., [as] when one lowers his voice in the same cases'.[22] In the second volume of his *Mémoires, ou Essais sur la musique* (1797), Grétry listed the affective qualities of eighteen keys, again basing his judgements on the sharp–flat principle, and describing A major as 'brilliant', B♭ as noble and *pathétique*.

A more Romantic perspective is evident some years earlier in a source already mentioned in relation to the development of the basset horn – Cramer's *Magazin der Musik* of 1783. An article in it by the physician and flautist J. J. H. Ribock offers his own personal feelings about each key, introducing analogous colours and inviting reactions from others. For him, A major is an 'expression of joy, cheerfulness, dancing: beautiful Saxon-green, refreshing aroma of lemons'. In Mozart's adopted city of Vienna, Schubart's celebrated table entitled 'Characteristics of the Keys' in his *Ideen zu einer Ästhetik der Tonkunst* was enormously influential on later musicians and drew comment from both Beethoven and Schumann. Schubart remarked: 'Every key is either coloured or uncoloured. Innocence and simplicity are expressed by uncoloured keys. Tender and melancholy feelings are expressed by flat keys, wild and strong passions by sharp keys.' For Schubart A major included 'declarations of innocent love, satisfaction with one's state of affairs; hope of seeing one's beloved again when parting; youthful cheerfulness and trust in God'.

The autumnal quality which many commentators have ascribed both to Mozart's Clarinet Quintet and to the Concerto arises in part from the use of a solo instrument which was commonly regarded as gentle and melancholy within a key which, for a variety of psychological and physical reasons, was generally thought to be brilliant and lively. Only in the nineteenth century did writers consider the implications of such a paradox for key characteristics as a whole. For example, Gottfried Weber noted in his *Versuch einer geordneten Theorie der Tonsetzkunst* (Mainz, 1817–21) that wind instruments became more shrill as they became higher-pitched, and so ' . . . it will be readily perceived . . . that the character which this or that key assumes, perhaps from the peculiar nature of wind instruments, may be exactly the reverse of that which the nature of string instruments imparts to it . . . these different mixtures and variations have the effect of imparting an individuality of character to the keys in a great variety of ways'.[23]

Mozart's choice of keys has been a subject for keen discussion in the work of Dent, Einstein, Abert, Keller, William Mann and many other scholars. For each tonality he developed a special orchestral palette, dependent on the practicality and effectiveness of the wind instruments as well as the coloration of the strings. Mozart avoided some options, such as the inclusion of C clarinets in his mature concertos and symphonies in C major. On the other hand, his encounter with the A clarinet seems to have provoked a replacement of a somewhat bland approach to A major with a tender, sensuous quality. Whilst it is true that the character of the musical material in the Quintet and Concerto contributes to their ambivalent emotional character, not least by means of prominent major–minor contrasts, the vocabulary of colour is an equally significant factor. Indeed, the extension of Stadler's basset clarinet in A must have increased the sweetness and gentleness of colour, thus contrasting even more markedly with the traditional brightness and vigour of the key of A major.

Mozart and the clarinet, 1788–91

Mozart's writing for the conventional clarinet had continued during 1788 in the E♭ Symphony K543 (dated 26 June), where in the absence of oboes the idiomatic duetting of clarinets in different registers within the Trio of the Menuet testifies to his enhanced level of intimacy with the instrument. Mozart's reorchestration K566 of Handel's *Acis and Galatea*, dating from November of the same year, serves to emphasise the increased profile of the clarinet within the full orchestral wind section; the setting of *Messiah* K572 in March 1789 presents a similar case. The Rondo 'Al desio, di chi t'adora' K577 was written in July 1789, to replace Susanna's aria 'Deh vieni, non

31

tardar' for a Vienna revival of *Figaro*, when the role was sung not by its creator Nancy Storace, but by Adriana Ferrarese del Bene. Significantly, Mozart included two virtuoso parts for *concertante* basset horns, marking an important revival of his interest in the instrument. From later in 1789 derives the Adagio fragment K580a, almost certainly for clarinet and three basset horns. Another related fragment (abandoned at the end of the exposition) is the F major Allegro K 580b for clarinet, basset horn and string trio, where the provision of an amenable tonality for the basset horn in F involves Mozart in the use of the C clarinet.

Così fan tutte, premièred on 26 January 1790, witnessed a radical development of the A clarinet's profile, though the B♭ also continued to develop in importance. When writing in E major, Mozart opted for A clarinets for the serene Terzettino 'Soave sia il vento', whereas in the Rondo 'Per pietà, ben mio', Fiordiligi's powerful emotions prompted an appearance of the more incisive B clarinet.[24] Mozart's growing awareness of the subtleties of different clarinet colours was to become an important feature of his work during the period leading up to the composition of the Clarinet Concerto the following year.

On 16 and 17 April 1791 the Stadler brothers took part in 'a grand symphony composed by Herr Mozart'.[25] It seems clear that this was the second version of the G minor Symphony K550, which was probably made immediately after completion of the autograph for a concert in 1788, since the watermarks of the additions match those of the original score.[26] Mozart's pragmatism in adapting his music to available resources transfers in this example from the theatre to the concert-room. G minor had not been a key which Mozart associated with the clarinet, and there is no doubt that the emotional effect of the symphony was radically altered by the addition of clarinets, even though they are allocated not quite all the prominent oboe material of the original version. Mozart's increasing involvement with the clarinet during 1791 is evident in both his operas from that year, *Die Zauberflöte* and *La clemenza di Tito*.

Masonic symbolism in *Die Zauberflöte* has been the subject of much discussion. Among five main indicators recently identified by Peter Branscombe is Mozart's dramatic usage of clarinets and basset horns.[27] Throughout the opera, prominent clarinets signify subject-matter of some importance, whilst basset horns denote ritualistic solemnity of a kind already observed in music from the mid-1780s. 30 September 1791 was the evening of the first performance of *Die Zauberflöte* at the Theater auf der Wieden in Vienna, when *La clemenza di Tito* was given its last performance in Prague.

Ex. 2

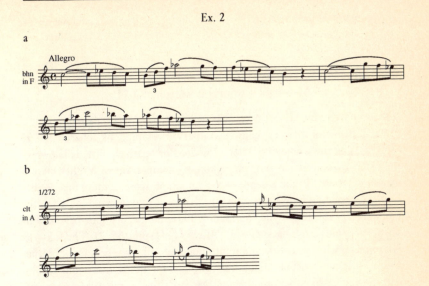

The two obbligato numbers in *La clemenza di Tito* offer a final glimpse of Stadler's favourite techniques immediately prior to the Clarinet Concerto. The solo writing for Bb basset clarinet and for basset horn incorporates slow, lyrical melody, chromatic passages, a wide variety of arpeggiated patterns and deep, rich sonorities. Yet these idioms are placed at the service of quite different dramatic contexts. In 'Parto, parto' Sesto asks Vitellia to make peace with him before he leaves, in an aria of great excitement and anxiety. Vitellia's Rondò 'Non più di fiori' is a musical and dramatic *tour de force*, which encompasses fear, despair and self-pity. The main Allegro theme bears a close thematic resemblance to the transition material in the first movement of the Clarinet Concerto, especially its reworking in the recapitulation (Exx. 2a and 2b).

Mozart arrived in Prague on 28 August and the opera's first performance took place on 6 September in honour of the coronation of Leopold II. Afterwards he returned to Vienna, but Stadler took part in several following performances.[28] After the last performance Mozart wrote to his wife at Baden on 7 and 8 October:

Meanwhile, I have had a letter which Stadler sent me from Prague. . . . Cries of 'Bravo' were shouted at Stodla [*sic*] from the balcony and even from the orchestra – 'What a miracle for Bohemia! – but indeed *I did my very best . . .*'. Stodla writes too that Süssmayr [deletion] . . . but I now see that he is an ass [–] I mean, not Stodla, who is only a bit of an ass – but [name deleted, presumably Süssmayr], why he is a full-blown ass. . . . Do urge Süssmayr to write something for Stadler, for he has begged me very earnestly to see to this.[29]

Mozart's autograph sketch, K621b

The same letter by Mozart notes that he had his manservant Joseph bring a black coffee and that he enjoyed a marvellous pipe of tobacco before orchestrating the whole of Stadler's Rondo. But relatively little is known of the Concerto's gestation and completion, by comparison with other mature works of Mozart. In the absence of the autograph score, a surviving 199-bar sketch for the first movement is an especially valuable source. Housed in the Rychenberg-Stiftung, Winterthur, since 1951, the twenty-four-page manuscript is reproduced in facsimile in *NMA* V/14/4, pp. 165–76. The solo part is complete, with some first violin tutti material and some bass line, together with a little inner detail. Orchestral scoring is for flutes, horns and strings, without the bassoons so prominent in Mozart's final version. Most extraordinarily, the first 179 bars are for basset horn in G, with accompaniment in G and D, but from bar 180, where the writing becomes darker and smaller, as if a new pen had been taken at that point, the accompaniment is a tone higher (in E at this point, not D); clearly at this stage Mozart had changed his mind and wanted the piece to be in A.[30] There are some further tiny differences from the finished Concerto K622 in the string parts at bars 98 and 195.

Mozart's initial choice of instrument may appear somewhat recondite, though the basset horn in G achieved more popularity in the eighteenth century than extant repertoire might suggest, and only after 1800 became almost as little known as the basset clarinet. The basset horn in G was chosen by Gerber in 1790 to illustrate the instrument's range, and even in 1829 Gottfried Weber was aware of it as a rarity.[31] The content of the discussions which must have taken place between Mozart and Stadler prior to the commencement of the Concerto is surely lost for ever.[32] Since both Mozart and Stadler were highly pragmatic musicians, it seems certain that Stadler had fitted a chromatic extension to his basset horn in G or at least that the idea was in his mind. Details of its design remain unknown. The choice of the smaller size of basset horn would imply a slightly more penetrating vibrant sound than its more mellow counterpart in F, though more gentle than any of the clarinets. As a key, G major was reckoned to have less character than A, Galeazzi (1796) regarding it as 'innocent, simple, unemotional, indifferent and of little effect', whilst Schubart characterised it as 'everything rustic, idyllic and lyrical, every calm and satisfied passion, every tender gratitude for true friendship and faithful love, – in a word, every gentle and peaceful emotion of the heart is correctly expressed by this key', adding, 'What a pity that because of its seeming lightness it is so greatly neglected nowadays'. Undoubtedly, the change of instrument and key to A substantially altered the relationship of solo and tutti in terms of colour, especially if the change to higher horn crooks is taken into account, together with the different characteristics of the strings. On the other hand, the tonal change in the solo part must have been far less than would have occurred between the more common basset horn in F and clarinet in B♭.[33]

Köchel's catalogue merely listed K621b under his entry for the Clarinet Concerto, but Einstein ascribed it to late 1789, as K584b, during the period of the Quintet. More recently, *NMA* and later editions of Köchel have favoured a dating within 1791, immediately prior to the Clarinet Concerto; this date is now preferred by Alan Tyson.[34] He has observed that the watermark on pages 1–6 of K621b indicates a type of paper used not only in 1784 and later, but also in 1791 (e.g. for the Dances K609). Pages 7–12 have a watermark traceable from 1785, of a type found in four pages of *Die Zauberflöte*. Thus, Tyson's previous suggestion of an earlier date for K621b – perhaps even 1787 – is theoretically possible, though less likely on stylistic grounds;[35] this dating would imply that it was Mozart's work on the Concerto which inspired Stadler to develop the basset clarinet, and that K621b pre-dates the Clarinet Quintet. But the very change of solo instrument at bar 180 of the manuscript, together with the simultaneous change of quill, might be indicative of such a passage of time. Despite the value of K621b as an autograph source, Mozart's initial choice of basset horn in G raises a number of as yet unanswered questions. But in his eventual scoring and choice of A major, Mozart was able to intensify the wide range of expression already evident within the Clarinet Quintet, whilst introducing a new virtuoso element appropriate to the concerto genre.

First performances of the Concerto

In Mozart's own catalogue of his works, the Clarinet Concerto remains undated, but is listed between *Die Zauberflöte* (28 September) and *Eine kleine Freymaurer-Kantate* (15 November). However, it seems clear (if not quite proven) that its première was given by Stadler at his concert at the Prague National Theatre on 16 October. It is likely that Stadler had been in Vienna during the fortnight since the performance of *La clemenza di Tito* in Prague on 30 September. Nissen's biography of Mozart (p. 684) states: 'For this same Stadler Mozart composed in October a concerto for the clarinet, gave to him the composition and travelling money to Prague, and made certain that he would make use of it there'. Rudolph Procházka's *Mozart in Prag* states:

Stadler went in any case for the purpose of concertizing to Prague, because he had a solo concert on 16 October 1791 in the National Theatre. In the government documents, from which Hr. Köpl, chief city archivist, kindly conveyed to me an excerpt from the police reports of permits given to concertizing artists on October 13 (document no. Gb-z. 30. 378): 'Anton Stadler, Royal chamber musician from Vienna, received, after payment of two florins to the poor fund, the permission to give on 16 October a concert of music in the Royal *Altstädter Theater*'.[36]

In 1791 Stadler requested a year's leave from Vienna, and it seems conceivable that he did not return there after his Prague concert.[37] Poulin (1991) has traced his subsequent European tour, on which at least one performance of the Mozart Concerto has been documented; there were surely several more. Reviews and programmes illustrate reaction both to Stadler's playing and to his new instrument. The tour took Stadler via Berlin to the Baltic coast, incorporating the following concert schedule:

> 31 January 1792: Berlin
> 23 March 1792: Berlin
> 4 May 1792: Warsaw
> 11 September 1792: Warsaw[38]
> 27 February 1794: Riga[39]
> 5 March 1794: Riga
> 21 March 1794: Riga
> 13 May 1794: St Petersburg
> 16 September 1794: Lübeck
> 27 September 1794: Lübeck
> 29 November 1794: Hamburg
> 20 December 1794: Hamburg
> 12 September 1795: Hanover

It is clear from the Berlin *Musikalisches Wochenblatt* of January 1792 that Stadler was heard by the public as well as at court:

Herr Stadeler, clarinettist from Vienna. A man of great talent and recognised as such at court, where he has already been heard on various occasions. His playing is brilliant and bears witness to his assurance. Overall, however, his playing lacks that ingratiatingly soft tone and tasteful delivery with which Herr Tausch . . . so often delights his listeners. Herr Stadeler has extended his instrument by the addition of keys; however, the benefit from the added keys, which make the instrument almost overloaded with keys, would not appear to be considerable.[40]

Other advertisements draw attention to the softer tone of Stadler's new instrument, and also to its range of four full octaves.

Poulin (1991) notes that the Mozart Clarinet Trio K498 was played on 29 November 1794. The Hanover programme mentions that the basset horn was also altered by Stadler. Most significantly, Poulin discovered from programme material that the second Riga concert included the Mozart Concerto, its first documented performance.[41] The programme also included the Süssmayr Concerto alluded to in Mozart's letter of 7/8 October 1791. This work was previously thought to have remained in draft, there being two sketches extant in the British Library for a first movement in D, clearly intended for basset clarinet in A (but without inclusion of the chromatic basset notes *c#* and *d#*). The earlier sketch is undated, but Alan Tyson has discovered it to be on Bohemian paper with a watermark identical to that used by Mozart in completing *La clemenza di Tito* in Prague in September 1791. Süssmayr was indeed present there at the coronation festivities for Leopold II. The second draft of the Concerto is dated Vienna li [no day] Jan [1]792.[42]

Stadler finally returned to Vienna in July 1796, where he gave a concert the following September.[43] Further performances of the Mozart Concerto have not yet come to light. On 10 April 1797 the Stadlers performed a new double concerto by Casimir Antonio Cartellieri, whilst on 22 and 23 December of the same year Anton played the obbligato in an aria from Süssmayr's cantata *Der Retter in Gefahr*. On 29 March 1798 Stadler played the basset horn obbligato (presumably 'Non più di fiori') to an aria sung by Frau Josepha Dušek. The following year he was pensioned, but according to Pamela Weston continued to play in the opera orchestra.[44] There were further concerts on 23 December 1805 and 31 March 1806 including the aria from Paer's *Sargino* sung by Madame Campi and accompanied by Stadler on the basset clarinet. The Viennese Staats-Schematismus for 1807–8 shows that Stadler once again played in the court orchestra at that time. He died from consumption on 15 June 1812 in unaccountable poverty.[45]

In the autumn of 1799 Stadler was asked by the Hungarian Count Georg Festetics of Kesthely am Plattensee to respond to sixteen questions that would serve as the basis of the establishment of a music school. Stadler's reply, dated 10 June 1800, was entitled *Musick Plan* and encompasses such topics as study schedules, accommodation, staffing, repertoire, curriculum, aesthetics, history of style and library provision.[46] Stadler insisted that every music student should study for an average of six years and learn basic principles through singing, whatever the quality of his voice. The discursive sections are laced with quotations from the classics and embody some really sound advice. A large bibliography mentions a clarinet method soon to be written; this has not surfaced. Such proof of Stadler's intelligence and culture has been ignored in favour of censure by Mozart's biographers arising from his allegedly dubious financial dealing and loose living. Evidence for this amounts to Constanze Mozart's letter (1800) to the publisher André, a story related by Nissen which derives from Constanze's sister, Sophie Haibl, and an inventory of Mozart's estate which cites Stadler as owing 500 florins.[47]

The nineteenth century

Around the year 1801 three sets of parts for the Concerto were published almost simultaneously:

(1) Concerto / pour / Clarinette / avec accompagnement d'Orchestre / composé par / W. A. Mozart / Oeuvre 107 /. . . No.1595. / . . . / Offenbach s/m. / chez Jean André / Umpfenbuch fecit.

(2) No. . . . [?] / Concerto / Pour Clarinette principalle / Deux Violons Alto et Basse / 2 Flutes 2 Bassons 2 Cors / Composés Par / W. A. Mozart / Opera . . . /A Paris / chéz SIEBER pere Editeur de Musique rue Honoré la porte Cochere / entre les rues Vielles Etuves et d'Orleans. No. 85. / . . . (Plate No. 1552)

(3) No. 7 / Concert / pour Clarinette / avec accompagnement / de / 2 Violons, 2 Flûtes, 2 Bassons, 2 Cors, / Viola et Basse / par / W. A. MOZART / . . . / Chez Breitkopf & Härtel / à Leipsic. / . . . (Catalogue No. 59)

All three editions contain the same transcription of the Concerto, for normal A clarinet. It has been suggested (but not proven) that André himself might have been responsible for the arrangement, though the Clarinet Concerto was not among the collection of autograph scores he bought from Mozart's widow in January 1800.[48] The André edition differs from the others in its expression markings and even in terms of actual notes (excluding obvious misprints); it is perhaps the most reliable, in so far as such a term can be used in relation to a transcription. Furthermore, it seems clear that the Sieber derives from the Breitkopf, since it contains additional printing errors as well as those which are common to both sources.

In 1802 a review of the Breitkopf and Härtel edition appeared in the *Allgemeine Musikalische Zeitung* (volume 4, cols. 408–13). This review (translated in Appendix 1) gained wide publicity through an article of 1967 by Ernst Hess, who believed its author to be Friedrich Rochlitz, editor of *AMZ*.[49] It contains an enthusiastic appreciation of the Concerto and early appraisal of its technical difficulties. The writer had before him an original score or (as Hess surmised) a copy, a fact which raises hopes for its eventual rediscovery. In discussing the anonymous transcription for normal A clarinet, the writer remarked:

And in this way very many places have been transposed and changed. . . . Whereas nowadays such clarinets descending to low *c* must still be counted among rare instruments, one is indebted to the editors for these transpositions and alterations for the normal clarinet, although the concerto has not exactly gained thereby. Perhaps it would have been just as well to have published it in the original version and to have marked these transpositions and alterations in smaller notes.

This is a far-sighted comment on the role of editor, and naturally the musical illustrations and references in the review have been an important source for the reconstruction of Mozart's text.

During the nineteenth century the transcription for normal A clarinet became established as the performing version of the Concerto, though in Leipzig the 1817 edition of the Whistling *Handbuch der Musikalischen Litteratur* made a footnote reference (p. 196) to the 1802 *AMZ* review.[50] Pamela Weston discovered nineteenth-century performances of the Concerto by Bernhard Crusell (1802, 1804), Simon Hermstedt (1809, 1814), Wilhelm Barth (1815, 1821), Feldt (1823), C. Rakemann (1836), Wenzel Farník (1837), Anton Friedlowsky (1837), Thomas Willman (1838), Carl Baermann (1843), Bernhard Landgraf (1853), Friedrich Wilhelm Grosse (1855) and Richard Mühlfeld (1891).[51] Most performances took place in Germany, although there were two celebrated performances in England, both of which were received with serious reservations about the music.

Willman's London première at a Philharmonic Concert in 1838 received the following notice in the *Musical World* of 22 March (pp. 198–9):

The novelty it will be seen was the concerto *said to be* [original italics] the composition of Mozart, and proceeding from the laboratory of M. André of Offenbach, who, like M. Fétis with the compositions of Beethoven, has proved himself an industrious stepfather to the posthumous compositions of Mozart. We look with great suspicion on those novelties from the pens of older composers long deceased. In the present instance we shall do no more than give the reasons for and against the authenticity of this concerto, leaving our readers to decide for themselves. In favour of it being a genuine production, M. André is said to have purchased most of the composer's MSS – that it has been twenty years in the possession of Mr Williams, the celebrated clarionet player, late of Hereford, but now of London; that the first and last movements are old-fashioned in their structure and are without the passages – the divisions upon the diminished chord – which, to speak technically, lie across the instrument, and which it is for modern ingenuity to invent, and consummate tact to overcome and successfully to execute; and that the middle movement, the *Andante* in D major, displays the voluptuous sensibility, the contrapuntal skill with which Mozart, and he alone, could have invested it.

On the other side, it is alleged that there is nothing in the concerto which internally stamps it as the production of Mozart, save the *andante*. The first movement is 'the music of the peruke'; in its terse and sententious phrases we discover the wig-tailed *maestro* of the last century; but there is nothing which M. André could not have written himself, more especially having the concerted composition for the clarinet in the same key, a recognized production of Mozart, for his model. We allude to the quintet in A, performed several times during the concerts of the past seasons. The *finale* of the present concerto is decidedly vulgar, and as far as a single hearing may be depended on, affords evident traces of haste and inexperience. The *andante* has the true Mozartian flavour about it, and the strikingly unexpected change to F sharp minor which occurs in the second part of the *motif*, puts it, we think, beyond doubt, that, at least, this movement may be considered the composition of the great master. Mr Willman had undertaken a task of great difficulty. The *soli* passages are very extended (a fact which, at all events, forbids us to suppose the concerto to have been a late work of Mozart), and how Mr Willman triumphed over them with so much ease passes ordinary comprehension. The *andante* was deliciously performed and excited great interest. The *cadenza* was a sorry affair and evidently written by one who was no clarinet player. The blossoms of imitation and the change into B flat [*sic*], might have been turned to good account, but as Mr Willman gave it, the whole was too sketchy to prove interesting or agreeable.

The programme on that occasion also featured ensembles from operas composed by Cimarosa and von Winter a mere five years after Mozart's Concerto. The evening began with a performance of Beethoven's Eighth Symphony, 'so elegant, fairy-like, spirited and grand that it may be said to have *killed* all that followed'.

Willman was typical of his period in giving many more performances of the obbligati to 'Parto, parto' and 'Non più di fiori' than of the Concerto. The popularity of Mozart's music was much more selective than today, and in any event wind concertos were becoming less fashionable. When Grosse, clarinettist for the Gentlemen's Concerts in Manchester, gave a concert in

1855, Charles Hallé wrote in his diary: 'A clarinet concerto in A by Mozart was capitally played by our excellent clarinettist, Grosse. The composition, although by Mozart, is such a grandfatherly production and so lengthy that the finale had to be left out, not to try the patience of the public beyond endurance.'

In 1916 Oscar Street described the Quintet and the Concerto as 'monuments for all time' and 'vivid examples of the masterly way in which Mozart had grasped the capabilities of the instrument'. His lecture continued:

Most of you are no doubt familiar with the quintet, but the concerto is, alas! very seldom heard nowadays. I find that it has not been played at a Philharmonic Concert since Willman played it in 1838, and as a Fellow of that honourable old Society, I should like to place on record my regret at the neglect of such a beautiful work. I have only heard it played once in its entirety, and that was by Mr Charles Draper in the early days of the Beecham Orchestra.[52]

Though the Concerto was not at this time associated with the basset clarinet, awareness of the instrument was kept alive by 'Parto, parto', whose obbligato continued to be published with its original range to low c, for example in the Breitkopf and Härtel Collected Edition of 1882. There were references to the instrument in C. F. Pohl's books on the Tonkünstler-Societät (1871) and on Haydn (1875–82), whilst Oscar Street realised in 1916 that 'Parto, parto' was intended for an extended clarinet.

The age of recordings, pre-1950

When clarinet concerto movements began to be recorded during the first decade of the twentieth century, Weber rather than Mozart won immediate favour. By 1926 Mozart's Quintet (as well as Brahms's Trio and Quintet) had been committed to disc, chamber music for clarinet finding a number of interpreters in the inter-war period. The first complete recording of the Mozart Concerto was made only in 1929 by Haydn Draper (Brunswick 20076–8).[53] It was also recorded on 78s by the Italian Luigi Amodio with the Berlin Municipal Orchestra, by François Etienne and the Hewitt Chamber Orchestra and by Reginald Kell with the London Philharmonic.[54] A celebrated recording by the Viennese clarinettist Leopold Wlach followed in 1949.

Even at this period the extended clarinet was scarcely associated at all with Mozart's Concerto, though it found a mention in Tenschert's 1930 article relating to the fragment K581a. Oscar Kroll knew of the instrument in the

41

mid-1930s during the preparation of his book *Die Klarinette*, to which he wrote a preface in 1944, but which was published posthumously only in 1965.[55] Donald Tovey was confused by the clarinet compass in one of the quintet fragments, remarking in 1939 that it 'breaks off soon after Mozart has betrayed a manifest absence of mind as to the downward compass of the instrument'.[56] But as early as 1941 future members of the Galpin Society had become aware of the *AMZ* review, more than a quarter of a century before it was reprinted.[57]

4

Stadler's clarinet and its revival

Viennese clarinets and basset horns

A variety of evidence testifies to the pre-eminence of Vienna in the development of the classical clarinet. Schubart in 1784–5 singled out the city as an important centre of clarinet manufacture (together with Nuremberg, Munich, Hamburg and Berlin), whilst Backofen *c.* 1803 stated in his tutor that the finest basset horns were made in Vienna. The homogeneous but distinctive sound-quality of classical Viennese clarinets arises from a number of characteristic and progressive features. In Appendix 2 Nicholas Shackleton discusses and lists various instruments whose design and provenance make them especially relevant to a study of the Mozart Concerto. A recent report on the playing response of the surviving B♭ clarinet by Stadler's collaborator Theodor Lotz (1748–92) confirms its special qualities:

. . . Playing on this Lotz clarinet, complete in all its components, was certainly a gratifying experience. It probably possessed the largest, 'thickest' sound of any eighteenth-century clarinet that I tested, rounded and woody throughout its entire range, in the tradition of the best German players (and instruments!) of today. Particularly impressive were the good intonation between the registers and the evenness of scale in the lower register. Both are significant in light of Mozart's extensive use of this register. The dynamic range and timbral quality of this Lotz clarinet are no doubt related to the very large bore size (between 15.00 and 15.05 mm) found on this instrument, one of the largest I found on any eighteenth-century clarinet and large even by today's standards. Perhaps this was a distinctive feature of Viennese clarinets, for an A clarinet by Kaspar Tauber in the Shackleton collection is very similar in this respect. It would certainly give credence to Shackleton's statement that the Bohemian clarinet of Mozart's time was already more highly evolved than elsewhere. . . . [1]

The Lotz clarinet incorporates a number of advanced technical features, including exceptionally well-designed keywork.

To complement these organological developments, it has been further established that the Austro-German performing tradition was among the first to embrace the modern practice of playing with the reed against the lower rather than the upper lip. Evidence for this includes the position of the mouthpiece stamp on the Lotz clarinet.[2] France and England were slower to adopt this technique, and in 1808 an anonymous commentator 'M' in the *Allgemeine Musikalische Zeitung* urged any clarinettists still playing in the French manner to switch, asking how it was possible to cultivate a soft and expressive tone when the reed was in contact with the teeth. Though only a single clarinet by Lotz survives, there are several very similar instruments by Raymund Griesbacher (1751/2–1818), with whom the Stadlers played basset horn trios.[3] In Prague an important maker was Franz Doleisch (1748/9–1806), whose instruments appear all to have been dated by him.[4] The normal configuration of all these instruments was five – sometimes six – keys.

It is rather curious that a greater number of Viennese basset horns than clarinets have survived in excellent condition, a situation which surely arises from their comparative lack of use. Basset horns pitched in G are extremely scarce, apart from the early sickle-shaped specimens by the Mayrhofers of Passau. However, basset horns in F (of the later angular design with two limbs joined at a knee) are well represented by both Lotz and Griesbacher. All their surviving instruments have only the two diatonic basset notes *c* and *d* (see Appendix 2).

At this date an eight-keyed configuration was the norm, including the usual mechanism for *c* and *d*. As already noted, Doleisch was responsible for some notable aspects of design not characteristic of Viennese instruments.

Surviving basset clarinets as evidence

During an era when instrument manufacture was far less standardised than we can imagine, extended clarinets were made to a variety of designs. The relationship of Stadler's newly developed *Bass-Klarinet* to the basset horn is difficult to determine; in his autograph fragments Mozart denotes it simply as 'clarinet', implying something other than simply a small basset horn in A or B♭. Therefore the Mayrhofer basset horn in A (Appendix 2, no. 1) can be regarded as a basset clarinet only with the benefit of hindsight and within the broadest of definitions, since it is of identical design to two basset horns in G from the same workshop. The anonymous instrument in Paris (no. 6) presents a later version of this category, effectively a small version of the by now angular basset horn.

The Paris instruments no. 2 and no. 3 have in the past been identified as a pair of *clarinettes d'amour*, though they are furnished with large, flared bells, rather than the bulbous type characteristic of the genre; their completely straight main bore incorporates an extension to *c* (without *d*), representing an important early amalgam of clarinet and basset horn.[5] The anonymous curved instrument in Berlin (no. 4) also has a conventionally shaped bell and the extension as part of the main bore.

A third category, represented by the Eisenbrandt (no. 7, Fig. 4.1) and Strobach (no. 5) instruments, illustrates the grey area between basset clarinet, basset horn and *clarinette d' amour*; both (as well as no. 8) are furnished with an angled bulbous bell, yet neither has a *Buch* containing the extension. The Strobach, whose pitch (A) is stamped on the upper joint, has until recently been regarded as a basset horn, since it is furnished with the knee characteristic of that instrument. The straight-bored Eisenbrandt is similar in shape to a larger six-keyed instrument in the Royal College of Music, London (RCM 87), catalogued as an anonymous (? German) early nineteenth-century basset horn in F.[6]

Stadler's design

A detailed if somewhat ambiguous description of Stadler's clarinet was written by Friedrich Bertuch in 1801:

Herr Stadler, a great virtuoso of several wind instruments, presented himself at one of the concerts performed by amateurs in the Augarten. He played a clarinet with modifications of his own invention. His instrument does not, as is usual, run straight down to the bell. About the last quarter of its length is fitted with a transverse pipe from which the projecting bell [*hervorragende Öffnung*] flares out further. The advantage of this modification is that the instrument gains more depth by this means and in the lowest notes resembles the horn.[7]

Bertuch formed the basis for the following fanciful description in Wilhelm Schneider's *Historische-technische Beschreibung der musikalischen Instrumente*:[8] 'Stadler, royal musician in Vienna, made some modifications to his clarinet in 1801; he lengthened and bent the bell sideways and thus added four low notes, that is *d♯*, *d*, *c♯* and *c*. It seems, however, that this invention was not very widespread, since few such instruments are seen.' Heinrich Welcker's *Musikalische Tonwerkzeuge*[9] has a more accurate date for the invention: 'The Viennese court musician Stadler (around 1790) lengthened the instrument and bent it sideways somewhat at the bell, in the same way as the bent flute of Midas . . . '.

Pamela Poulin observed that while Bertuch's description might apply to the *Buch* of a basset horn, ' . . . it would seem unlikely that an informed reviewer would mistake a basset horn for a clarinet . . . '.[10] Her subsequent retracing

Fig. 4.1. Basset clarinet in C (after 1800) by Johann Benjamin Eisenbrandt
reproduced by kind permission of Eric Hoeprich

Fig. 4.2. Basset clarinet in A (1994) by Eric Hoeprich
reproduced with his kind permission

of Stadler's steps throughout Europe uncovered evidence which apparently justifies her earlier remark. For Stadler's programmes for his 1794 Riga concerts were found to contain an engraving of his own special instrument. Although in size and scope this illustration has the character of a thumb-nail sketch, it gives sufficient information to enable a basset clarinet of similar design to be created (Fig. 4.2). The result closely resembles the Eisenbrandt basset clarinet, which may in turn have been directly inspired by Stadler's invention.[11] The two instruments seem plausibly to reflect Bertuch's description. Powerful support for Poulin's evidence comes from an incomplete letter dated 2 May 1795 from Stadler to Daniel Schütte, music director of the theatre at Bremen, to arrange performances there and to commission from the maker Tietzel 'eine neue Art Clarinette d'amour' ('a new type of *clarinette d'amour*') to his own specifications.[12]

If it can be assumed that the Riga engraving was drawn by someone with a knowledge of Stadler's instrument, the distinction in design between his clarinet and basset horn finally becomes clearer. A relevant point here is that the mechanism for the four basset notes would have been easier for a maker to achieve on a straight tube, rather than on the *Buch* of the basset horn. Given the pragmatism of both Mozart and Stadler, this may have been a factor in the change of Mozart's solo instrument from basset horn in G to basset clarinet in A during the gestation of the virtuoso Clarinet Concerto. Details of the collaboration between the maker Theodor Lotz and Stadler in developing the new clarinet remain uncertain. As we noted on page 27, there is no evidence to suggest that Stadler was himself a maker; indeed, his communication relating to Tietzel might tend to suggest that Stadler commissioned rather than actually built instruments.

Stadler's concert announcements make clear that his instrument could play a full four octaves (c–c''''), the range of the solo part of Süssmayr's concerto sketch. If there was any disagreement between Mozart and Stadler concerning the capabilities of the clarinet, it must surely have related to the extreme high register, which Mozart studiously avoided. The *AMZ* article of 1808 praised Mozart's appreciation of the clarinet's beauty of tone, approved his virtual avoidance of f''' and g''', and proceeded to criticise the extremes of tessitura favoured by the contemporary virtuoso and composer Franz Tausch. Relevant to a discussion of the clarinet's response in the low register is the question of the degree of mechanism fitted to Stadler's instrument, details of which cannot be gleaned from the Riga sketch. The Berlin *Musikalisches Wochenblatt* describes the instrument as 'almost overloaded with keys' (see page 37) but there is no reason to suppose that this does not relate to the basset extension.

There has been much debate as to whether the main part of Stadler's instrument was based on the five-keyed configuration in general currency. In his favourite chalumeau register, *b*, *c#'* and *eb'* were especially difficult to produce on this type of clarinet, though for many clarinettists additional keys to facilitate such notes were regarded as hazardous in relation both to technique and maintenance. Lefèvre noted in his tutor of 1802 that a sixth key for *c#'* was indispensable, since otherwise the note was indistinguishable from *d'*. By 1808 the writer in *AMZ* was recommending at least nine keys to avoid dull and scarcely useable notes, citing Mozart's Concerto as evidence and addressing the usual counter-argument by stating that his own new clarinet had been played daily for nine months without needing a single repair. The handling of a more complex instrument, with its increased risk of leakage from keypads, was a challenge that Stadler was clearly well equipped to tackle. In his *Musick Plan* he (like Backofen) was at pains to emphasise the importance of instrument maintenance, which must have been especially important in the case of the basset clarinet. Stadler's progressive approach to clarinet design and the predisposition of players of the basset horn to add one or two extra keys are important elements in the equation. Mozart's confidence in the chalumeau register sometimes seems to emphasise an apparently difficult note (as in the Concerto first movement, bar 118), perhaps suggesting the presence of a key or double hole for its production. The relationship of the phenomenal Stadler to the norms represented by surviving instruments and tutors is now almost impossible to determine, though players of our own time have proved that mastery of cross-fingerings and shadings can produce remarkable results from minimal keywork.

The nineteenth century

Although there is no documentary evidence that the basset clarinet was played by anyone other than Stadler during his lifetime, there is some evidence that its use was not confined to him. In the *Kaiserliche Wiener Zeitung* of 2 April 1803 Franz Scholl advertised

... his newly designed and considerably improved wind instruments, a portion of which are of his own invention. His clarinet (in Bb or C) extended two tones lower, that is to low c, which since one has the tonic note for cadences, always produces a good effect. Moreover, his clarinets strongly recommend themselves by their good construction, by their good intonation and by a new way in which the keys are mounted.[13]

Scholl claimed to have received a patent on his inventions (not including the basset clarinet) from his Imperial Majesty, though on at least two occasions in 1794 and 1799 his attempt to fill Lotz's position as court instrument maker after the latter's death was rejected by the emperor. Scholl, it may be noted, was offering basset clarinets in C as well as B♭, with diatonic rather than chromatic extension.

The basset clarinet by Bischoff (no. 9) was made for the Darmstadt court, whose musicians included the clarinettist Backofen.[14] Poulin believes that this instrument may have been used for the first Darmstadt performance of *La clemenza di Tito* for the opening of the Hoftheater on 26 October 1810, though Shackleton has postulated a date of manufacture closer to 1840. The provision of a fully chromatic extension (not required in the B♭ basset clarinet repertoire) has been explained by the survival in the Darmstadt Theater Bibliothek until World War II of a score and parts to a B♭ version of Mozart's Clarinet Concerto, as well as a piano rehearsal reduction.[15] It must have been a performance of *La clemenza di Tito* which inspired the much later anonymous high-pitched and diatonically extended B♭ basset clarinet (no. 10) now in Oxford. By the time it was built, during the second half of the nineteenth century, musical literature was exhibiting some vagueness about Stadler's contribution to the history of the clarinet: in 1869, Hanslick wrote that Anton and his brother 'made a few improvements to the clarinet', whilst Mendel in his lexicon of 1878 added only that 'they contributed, through the addition of keys to their instruments, to its essential improvement'.[16]

The twentieth-century revival

After its revival in 1950 the basset clarinet remained a minority interest amongst clarinettists for the next thirty years or so. Recordings of the traditional reading continued apace, with versions from Kell, Delécluse, Walton, de Peyer, Schönhofer, Goodman, de Wilde, Geuser, Lancelot and Brymer in the period up to 1960.[17] More than twenty years later, when David Etheridge came to compare eight celebrated recordings of the Concerto – by Hasty, Marcellus, Gigliotti, Wright, Jettel, Delécluse, Brymer and Incenzo – all the interpretations he discussed were played on the conventional A clarinet.[18] As a reflection of the general situation in 1978, the list of re-created basset clarinets which formed part of the *NMA Kritischer Bericht* V/14/4 (Cassel, 1982), p. d/16, comprised a mere seven instruments.[19]

In 1950 Milan Kostohryz of the Prague Conservatory was the first to have a Boehm-system A clarinet extended by the Czech maker Rudolf Trejbal. The extra keys were designed for the right-hand thumb, and the top of the instrument furnished with a curved metal crook to facilitate playing position;

these features were transferred from the basset horn. Trejbal later constructed a German-system basset clarinet of similar design, which was illustrated in the English version of Oscar Kroll's book.[20] Gerhard Croll and Kurt Birsak subsequently made an attempt to take into account Bertuch's description of 1801 by commissioning from Otto Hammerschmidt a lower joint leading to a small bent barrel, which allowed the bell to 'project outwards'. Their instrument was illustrated in an article of 1969.[21] This was also the year of Alan Hacker's first London performance on a clarinet extended by Edward Planas. The instrument was described and illustrated in an article by Hacker.[22] At the same time a pioneering recording (Ex libris EL 16545) was made by Hans-Rudolf Stalder on a modern Boehm-system instrument by Arthur Uebel, using a reconstructed text by Ernst Hess. Little more than a decade later, basset clarinets in A began to be commercially available from the principal manufacturers.

Interest in reproducing an older style of clarinet began with Hans Deinzer's 1973 recording (BASF BAC 3001) on a generously mechanised boxwood instrument by Rudolf Tutz. Since that time, various designs have been re-created. In 1978 Tutz made for Stalder a basset clarinet closely related to the late eighteenth-century basset horn, with *Buch* and metal bell but without a knee.[23] This pattern has been favoured by some later players.[24] In contrast, Alan Hacker preferred to commission straight extensions of original clarinets, such as Edward Planas's modification of a mid-nineteenth-century clarinet by Dölling pictured by Jack Brymer, *Clarinet*, fig. 8. Hacker's 1985 recording of the Concerto was made on an early nineteenth-century clarinet by the English maker Thomas Key, modified and extended by Brian Ackerman. The Tauber A clarinet in the Shackleton collection provided the inspiration for the straight basset clarinet (with curved barrel) built for Antony Pay in 1984 by Edward Planas and Daniel Bangham.[25] Meanwhile, Kurt Birsak commissioned from Tutz a boxwood basset clarinet with straight bore and barrel, but with a metal bell projecting away from the player.[26] In the light of recent research, it seems likely that a projecting bulbous bell (as in Figs. 4.1 and 4.2) will become a feature of at least some of the boxwood basset clarinets created in the future.

5

Mozart's original text

The reconstruction

A reconstruction of Mozart's original text for basset clarinet was published in 1977 as part of the *Neue Mozart-Ausgabe*, since when performances on the extended instrument have gradually been winning widespread acceptance, both in the concert hall and in recordings. Because the *NMA* text is widely available for consultation, not every detail of the reconstruction process will be explored within this chapter. The two primary sources have already been identified, comprising (1) Mozart's own initial 199 bars from the autograph sketch K621b for basset horn in G, and (2) musical examples given in the 1802 *Allgemeine Musikalische Zeitung* review of the first Breitkopf and Härtel edition. These can be supplemented by internal evidence of orchestration and melodic shape.

With remarkable percipience, although without apparent knowledge of K621b or the *AMZ* review, George Dazeley in 1948 incorporated a list of emendations to the traditional text for normal clarinet, which contained the essential material for a complete reconstruction. The first modern performance of a basset clarinet version of the Concerto was given in Prague in 1951 by Milan Kostorhryz's pupil Josef Janous. Jiří Kratochvíl played the Quintet on a specially reconstructed instrument in 1956 and subsequently published a series of articles on Mozart's original texts for both pieces.[1] The year 1967 witnessed the publication of the seminal article by Ernst Hess, which drew attention to the *AMZ* review and addressed various problems in re-creating the text.[2] Shortly afterwards, Alan Hacker offered some further observations on the current state of research.[3] These various threads were drawn together in Franz Giegling's edition for the *NMA* volume V/14/4, containing both the traditional version for normal A clarinet, together with a reconstructed version for basset clarinet.[4] The separately published critical commentary contains a list of sources, as well as various further detailed information relating to the reconstruction of Stadler's instrument and the solo part.[5] Among its most valuable material is the complete German text of the 1802 *AMZ* review.

Ex. 3

Ex. 4

Primary evidence

Various types of basset writing are evident in Mozart's own hand within the autograph sketch K621b. For example, the contours of his original solo line at bars 1/91–2 (Ex. 3) incorporate dialogue between soprano and baritone registers of the clarinet.[6] The alberti figuration at bars 1/134–40 was originally intended to make extensive use of the written low notes c and d. The arpeggios at bars 1/145–7 were originally pitched an octave lower, and therefore excluded the high g''' required in the edited version of bar 147. Among the closing bars of the sketch is the wide-ranging passage from bar 1/186, which encompasses a range of three full octaves. Especially significant solo details elsewhere include the passage in Example 4. The deletions and changes probably followed a complaint from Stadler about the intractability of the initial group of semiquavers. It happens that Mozart's biographer Otto Jahn reported a dialogue between Stadler and the composer, which derives from the composer Sigismund Neukomm, and clearly relates to an awkward passage such as this, which Stadler asked to be altered: 'Have you the notes on your instrument?' 'Certainly they are on it.' 'Provided they exist it is your concern

Ex. 5

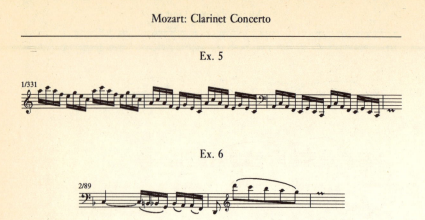

Ex. 6

to produce them.'[7] The evidence from surviving clarinets of the period is in fact that most notes but not all intervals between them are readily available.

The *AMZ* reviewer's illustrations duplicate some of the contexts in Mozart's autograph sketch, but also contribute some important information about the central portion (bars 45–58) of the Adagio, in which the basset register was originally prominent. The Rondo also yields a straightened arpeggio figure at bars 61–2. Bars 3/99–104 (and by implication 232–7) were originally an octave lower and nicely illuminate the qualities of the clarinet's different registers. Because the reviewer prints scarcely any examples from the solo part, but simply refers to page numbers and lines of the solo part of the edition (for normal A clarinet) under review, not all his indications relating to the original are totally unambiguous. But they are sufficient in number to encourage a number of deductions about suspicious contexts elsewhere.

Internal evidence

Important areas in the first movement include bars 1/331–3, which incorporate what in the traditional version appears to be a redundant repeated bar. Without doubt, this passage must have originally ranged over three octaves (Ex. 5). In the Adagio, the transposer-arranger appears to have covered his tracks more effectively than in the outer movements, although the contour in Example 6 (bars 2/89–90) seems by analogy with bars 2/85–6 (which it imitates) to have been altered to avoid the low *d*. The Rondo contains a variety of melodies which show evidence of transposition, including bars 65–8 and bars 77–81. Some arpeggios (such as bars 61–2 and 67) in the solo line must originally have been straightened out. It seems clear that the dialogue passage at bars 3/169–74 originally continued downward to incorporate the bottom

Ex. 7

Ex. 8

tonic, written *c*. Furthermore, the arpeggiated pattern at bars 3/311–13 was clearly originally an octave lower, and lies in an awkward register in the traditional version.

Ambiguities

Most contemporary performances on the basset clarinet incorporate all the restorations mentioned above, together with several others which are included in the *NMA* and have become established in common practice. Rediscovery of Mozart's score, however, would clarify a number of passages which to this day remain unclear. Ernst Hess was among commentators who recognised that a complete solution was beyond the scope of mere deduction, however astute and musical. For example, one might surmise (with Hess and *NMA*) that the contour of 1/299 was originally as in Example 7. If so, the arpeggiated figure which precedes it at bar 1/295 (Ex. 8) should surely be retained in its traditional broken form, especially since a parallel figure is contained within the obbligato to 'Parto, parto' in *La clemenza di Tito* (bars 80–2), suggesting a counsel of constraint. Hess rightly warns against transposition of every single possibility, which in some passages such as 1/216–20 would have a detrimental effect on the disposition of the harmony. In any event, precise details of reconstruction are not always self-evident; for 1/326, Example 9a is preferred by *NMA*, though Example 9b has seemed a more logical solution for some players.

In the central section of the Adagio already referred to (bars 45–58), the precise contour of bars 47 and 48 has remained controversial because of the failure of the *AMZ* writer to illustrate his reference with a musical example. In addition, the closing bars of this movement remain especially ambiguous.

Ex. 9

Ex. 10

The traditional version (Ex. 10a) makes perfect musical sense, though an octave transposition mid-way through bar 2/96 has seemed preferable to some players (Ex. 10b). Perhaps the sextuplet was originally a decoration of bar 93 and has itself been altered (Ex. 10c).

The Rondo has some passages (bars 197–9, 327) where the harmonic sense forbids downward transposition and would in any case result in unidiomatic conjunct chromatic movement in the basset register. But this movement contains a number of unresolved questions, such as the profile of the original contour at bars 110 and 243. Common consensus for the passage 146–53 has become the version at Example 11a, though *NMA* inexplicably opts for the

Ex. 11

Ex. 12

distorted Example 11b. At bars 165–8, instances of low *c* clearly need to be restored, but in which octave is the first beat of bar 165 (Ex. 12)? There are in fact one or two other ambiguities; for example, the termination of the trill at bar 317 is technically difficult on a period clarinet and may not have taken place within the lowest register. Recovery of Mozart's autograph or a contemporary copy would unlock the key to a number of small-scale textual mysteries.

The basset clarinet version assessed

For 150 years after publication of the earliest editions of the Concerto, the anonymous transcription for normal A clarinet formed the basis for every interpretation. It seems likely that the work will continue to be regularly performed in this guise. However, as a fuller knowledge of the work's background has become available, it has become customary and accepted practice in performances with normal clarinet to alter details of the

Ex. 13

transcription in order to achieve an enhanced solo contour. For example, bar 1/333 is now often played as in Example 13 (for which there is some evidence in surviving nineteenth-century manuscripts) rather than as a mere repeat of the previous bar (cf. Ex. 5). The necessity to be furnished with a special instrument solely for Mozart's Quintet and Concerto will always prove a barrier to performance on the basset clarinet, even within a climate where their musical quality is appreciated as never before. It is of course true that the well-known transcription for normal clarinet post-dates Mozart's composition by a mere ten years and that there is no actual *proof* of many details of the basset reconstruction, notwithstanding the evidence of the autograph sketch K621b and of the *AMZ* review. Some players have voiced the opinion that it was no accident that the basset clarinet never achieved widespread currency.[8] For at least one international figure the historical background is quite irrelevant; he has stated baldly that ' . . . I can do things with the "A" clarinet that I cannot do with the basset. I believe that these things add more to the overall performance than the few extra notes at the bottom.'[9] Lack of flexibility is indeed perceived by some as a negative feature of the Boehm-system basset clarinet. Furthermore, the challenge of building an instrument with acceptable intonation has sometimes been met less successfully with modern designs than boxwood reconstructions. Boehm-system basset clarinets have usually been designed so that every interval in the basset register can be slurred effectively, and not merely those required by Mozart; this demands a considerable amount of keywork surplus to what the Quintet or Concerto actually requires.

Despite all the difficulties relating to the basset clarinet – both in terms of performance and manufacture – we can now deduce sufficient detail of Mozart's original solo line to make its recapture a desirable aim. The amalgam of clarinet and basset horn for which Mozart wrote can inevitably be only partially represented by the normal A clarinet. In terms of colour, the increased length of any basset clarinet is likely to induce a special richness of tone, which is as characteristic of the instrument as its enhanced downward compass. What the modern-system basset clarinet can easily fail to deliver is a hint of the other-worldly, ethereal quality which we have already noted as part of the character of the eighteenth-century basset horn, deriving from its special acoustical peculiarities. The broad disagreement amongst modern manufacturers as to an appropriate design for today's basset horn is indicative of the difficulty of re-creating its unique tonal qualities.

Meanwhile, the special circumstances surrounding the composition of Mozart's Concerto and subsequent loss of the evidence have posed today's players an especially difficult conundrum in the re-creation of Mozart's masterpieces for the clarinet.

6

Design and structure

The discussion and analysis which follow may be read in association with any published score of the Concerto. However, a reconstruction for basset clarinet has been assumed throughout, so that editions for normal clarinet will not always correspond in every detail.

Background

From an early age Mozart found the concerto a natural mode of expression. During 1767 he arranged sonatas by other composers as concertos by adding orchestral accompaniments (K37 and K39–41), and he developed a number of structural innovations in the four original solo concertos (K175, 238, 246 and 271) which followed. After his move to Vienna a further trio of piano concertos (K413–15) dating from 1782 preceded the fourteen mature works (from K449 onwards) with which Mozart radically expanded the scope of the genre in terms of form, texture and idiom. In addressing this most highly organised of instrumental forms, blending sonata, concerto grosso, aria and ritornello, Mozart alone realised that the concerto could be transformed from mere entertainment into a structure which was quite distinct from the symphony or sonata. His dramatic music inevitably became an especially potent influence; as one celebrated writer has put it, 'Mozart found his greatest, most sincere range of expression in opera, and the most beautiful passages in the concertos are those wherein operatic Mozart quivers beneath the *galanterie* and virtuosity of the concert room'.[1]

Whereas piano concertos formed a consistently important part of Mozart's career as performer/composer, his concertos for wind instruments were always inspired by an association with a particular artist. Occasioned by special demand, they were never composed simply because inspiration dictated, and none was published during Mozart's lifetime. The Bassoon Concerto K191/ 186e (1774) was probably intended for Thaddäus von Dürnitz in Munich, whilst the Oboe Concerto K314/285d (1777) was for Guiseppe Ferlendis in

Salzburg, the Flute Concerto K313/285c and the reworking of K314/285d (1778) for De Jean in Mannheim, and the Concerto for Flute and Harp K299/297c (1778) for the Duc de Guines in Paris. All Mozart's woodwind concertos except for the Clarinet Concerto thus pre-date the Vienna years and exhibit many of the *galant* features which were characteristic of the genre at that time.

In Vienna it was Mozart's friendship with the horn player Joseph Leutgeb which yielded his only series of mature wind concertos. Recent research has re-dated the three E♭ horn concertos respectively 1783 (K417), 1786 (K495) and 1787 (K447), whilst the Concerto K412/386b in D has now been shown by Alan Tyson to date from 1791; indeed, Mozart was still working on its Rondo at the time of his death.[2] Mozart's writing for the natural horn remains a *tour de force*, with its mixture of effective idiom and colourful employment of stopped notes. But for all the range of expression contained within the horn concertos, there is as yet no hint of the sheer emotional breadth within the Clarinet Concerto.

Stylistic features

The melodic aspect of the Clarinet Concerto is dictated entirely by the character of the solo instrument, which after the opening tutti consistently holds centre stage. The upper part of the clarinet's compass inspires the greater proportion of thematic material, though the solo line frequently moves between low, middle and upper register. Rapid changes in tessitura often result in extremely wide leaps, regularly exceeding two octaves and (in the version for basset clarinet) sometimes extending to three. Mozart's additional use of the chalumeau register encompasses a variety of textures, including both purely melodic material as well as accompanying alberti figuration. This serves to relieve the predominantly homophonic character of the Concerto and contributes to a far richer variety of colour than is encountered within any of Mozart's other concertos for a single melody instrument. In addition to the consistently creative inner orchestral parts, principal material in each of the outer movements is subject to imitative treatment (for example, 1/25, 1/128, 1/316 and 3/196).

The choice of flutes, bassoons and horns as the orchestral wind section ensures a lucid, transparent sound which provides a perfect match for the tonal spectrum and articulations of the solo clarinet. The Concerto is not totally devoid of orchestral wind solos (cf. the flute at 3/77), but there is none of the independent wind serenading found in the piano concertos K482, 488 and 491, where the clarinets are such an important component. Instead, the Clarinet

Concerto maintains a consistent balance of orchestral colour through which the clarinet's various registers may be clearly heard.

Allegro

Each of the three movements shows the influence of structures developed within the piano concertos, though the balance of form and content is influenced to a considerable degree by the nature of the solo instrument. This may be clearly observed in the proportions of the first movement:

Orchestral ritornello:	bars 1–56
Solo exposition:	bars 57–154
Ritornello:	bars 154–71
Development:	bars 172–227
Ritornello:	bars 227–50
Recapitulation:	bars 251–343
Ritornello:	bars 343–59

The introductory nature of the opening ritornello is apparent not only in the character of the musical material, but in its relative proportion to the large-scale solo exposition. Comparison with the A major Piano Concerto K488 is instructive, where orchestral and solo expositions are considerably more finely balanced in length, extending to 66 and 70 bars respectively. Another aspect of the Clarinet Concerto's first movement which varies from the pattern established within the piano concertos is the insertion of a ritornello after the development (allowing the soloist pause for breath) and subsequent participation by the clarinet at the very beginning of the recapitulation. In addition, the Concerto is unusual for its date in offering no context for a genuine cadenza, in which it again differs from the precedent within Mozart's piano concertos. This was to become a standard feature of later virtuoso clarinet concertos by Weber and Spohr.

Orchestral ritornello. The principal theme which will later be subject to decoration by the clarinet is stated in bars 1–8 (see p. 81, strings) and answered by a tutti statement (bars 9–16) with some elaboration. Like many of Mozart's A major themes, this is characterised by a descending interval from the fifth degree of the scale, as at the beginning of the Piano Concerto K488, 'Ah taci, ingiusto core!' from *Don Giovanni* and the opening of the Clarinet Quintet. Nevertheless, its original conception in G major (cf. K621b) is a reminder that it is not exclusively an A major type. An important ritornello component (bars 16–19) follows, incorporating the characteristic rising seventh from bar 6. A semiquaver pattern which will later engage the soloist introduces a sequence (bars 20–2) featuring a degree of chromaticism and leading to a cadence on the dominant (bars 23–4). In place of a second orchestral subject the opening theme is treated canonically (bars 25–31, see p. 81) a device which will also recur later in the solo exposition and in the recapitulation. The remainder of the ritornello is concerned with tutti development of the main subject (bars 31–6), presentation of orchestral material which will later be combined with solo figuration (bars 39–43, introduced by bars 37–8), some chromatic orchestral material culminating in a perfect cadence at bars 48–9, and a codetta theme (bars 49–56) which will reappear after the solo exposition and at the close of the movement. Melodic continuity is a highly significant component of Mozart's late style, prominent in other works such as the Piano Concerto in B♭ K595. The opening ritornello of the Clarinet Concerto already demonstrates this linear dimension, where the effect of the (infrequent) perfect cadences remains disguised as a result of subtle interaction with various rhythmic devices.

Solo exposition. The clarinet elaborates the principal theme (bars 57–64), its entry striking for its reduced accompaniment of violins and (from the third bar) violas. The coloratura solo descant to the theme in tutti strings (bars 65–8) continues to a tonic cadence (bars 74–5) via some characteristic solo idioms, including wide-ranging arpeggios and a leap of two-and-a-half octaves (bar 70). The transition to the second subject at bar 100 is achieved in a quite remarkable way. Replacing the melodic figuration which regularly occurs at this part of the movement within Mozart's piano concertos is a change to a darker mood signalled by the orchestra (bars 76–7) and intensified in the clarinet line in A minor (from bar 78), which quickly moves via a dramatic chord of F minor (bar 81) to C major. Fingered as E♭ on a clarinet in A, this key has an individual colour characterised (on instruments of the period) by a greater proportion of cross-fingerings than thus far encountered in the solo part. (C major is used with similarly heightening effect at the beginning of the development of the first movement of the Clarinet Quintet.) The solo material from the upbeat to bar 86 is notable for its economical texture with first violins alone and for its slow harmonic rhythm. Before the appearance of the second subject there are various felicitous textural details, such as the juxtaposition of soprano and baritone solo registers (in Mozart's original version) at bars 91–2 (see Ex. 3, p. 53); after a move towards the dominant of E minor via an augmented-sixth chord at bar 93, semiquaver accompaniment to the two violin parts in the chalumeau register of the clarinet introduces an altogether new texture.

The immediate approach to the second subject is remarkable for its seamless quality, since the solo melody emerges without a break from the E minor imperfect cadence in the orchestra. The entire passage in bars 94–103 is rooted in B^7 harmony. The solo theme from bar 100 is initially more continuous than the first subject, drawing much of its expression from prominent use of dissonance on the main beats. Reduced accompaniment in the strings is again a characteristic feature. The sequential figuration from bars 20–2 of the ritornello provides material for continuation (bars 108–10), prior to a chromatic approach to a cadence in E major. From bar 115 the texture with first violins observed in bar 86 supports a solo line characterised by dialogue in the soprano and baritone registers of the clarinet in the key of C♯ minor. The first of the movement's two short cadential flourishes, at bar 127, occurs on a dominant seventh chord of E, inviting a short elaboration from the soloist. The exposition continues with a rescoring of ritornello material, now incorporating the soloist. The imitative entries at bars 25–30 recur at 128–33, followed in bars 134–7 by a transformation of bars 39–42 to include alberti figuration in the chalumeau register. This leads to a virtuoso culmination to the exposition, incorporating scales and arpeggios throughout the clarinet's range (bars 138–54). Its final cadence is approached via a characteristic upward-rising chromatic scale preceding the final trill.

As might be expected, the following ritornello derives from the opening orchestral material, now in the dominant. The active tutti texture of bars 16–23 is transposed to serve as bars 154–161, extended by a further new bar (bar 162) and then continuing in bars 163–71 with codetta material transferred from bars 48–56.

The development features the soloist throughout and is thus entirely melodic in texture. The tonality moves from E major through F♯ minor (bars 189–94) and D major (bars 199–200), then via B minor (bar 210) back to F♯ minor. Thematic content balances new ideas with elaboration of the principal material. The exposition's first subject forms a starting point for the nine-bar theme at bars 172–80, extended by semiquaver figuration in bars 180–6 to the climactic high note (written d''', sounding b''). The subsequent passage comprises various devices designed to exhibit special features of Stadler's instrument, including a dramatic three-octave melodic descent at bars 188–92, dialogue with the strings at bars 194–7 featuring the basset clarinet's lowest notes, and further theatrical demonstration of range at bars 198–9 against a full but *piano* wind chord. The soloist's continuation transposes the passage from bar 86 up a tone to D, incorporating dialogue with the chalumeau register but developing the material via some new chromaticisms to restore the development's main key, F♯ minor, at bar 215. The dramatic single-bar orchestral interjection reverts momentarily to the mood of bars 192–3, recalling in character (though not in content) the two-bar orchestral preface to the second subject in the exposition. This middle solo ends with some extremes of contrast. The four semibreves at bars 216–19 invite comparison with similarly stark contexts in Mozart's piano concertos, where some solo elaboration may have been intended. The passage, whose orchestral accompaniment recalls the dialogue at bars 194–7, is also remarkable for its *piano* dynamic and for its effective use of the Neapolitan chord in bar 216. The material at the end of this solo (bars 220–7) recalls the close of the exposition, also incorporating an interjection (bar 223) in the chalumeau register. A bridge to the *forte* dramatic orchestral ritornello is achieved by means of a chain of solo trills.

The following orchestral ritornello is the most dramatic in mood and comprises two principal elements. Bars 227–39 develop the forceful orchestral texture introduced in the interjection at bar 215 and are related melodically to the clarinet figuration at bar 95. A six-bar passage in F♯ minor is repeated in sequence in E minor, leading to a cadence in D at bar 239; the material incorporates various chromatic touches, together with some expressive suspensions from bassoons and cellos in their tenor register. The second element is made up of more familiar material; bars 16–22 in the initial ritornello form the basis of bars 239–45, with some minor melodic variation and a modification in bar 242 to propel the music towards the dominant of A major. The following orchestral cadential bars take elements from the solo figuration at bar 95 and the closing ritornello bar which occurs elsewhere in the movement at bars 55, 169 and 358.

The lead-in to the recapitulation bears a striking harmonic and melodic resemblance to the equivalent point in Mozart's Clarinet Quintet, beginning with a clarinet rising scale at bar 248 (replacing the Quintet's arpeggio), moving to a held solo note above a lead-in (bars 249–50) played by upper strings and bassoons. Notwithstanding the chromaticism of this passage, the effect is quite distinct from any parallel context within the piano concertos. The recapitulation maintains a close resemblance to the solo exposition, the material of the first subject virtually repeated (bars 251–69). However, the transition is transformed with especially poignant effect (see Ex. 2b, p. 33), beginning (bars 270–4) as if to repeat the exposition material, though with heightened intensity in the tessitura of the accompaniment. The continuation (bars 275–82) develops the second solo bar (bar 273), moving from A minor through C major, E minor and D minor. The C major theme originally played in bars 86–94 is not recapitulated, having formed an important part of the development material. The passage from bars 94 to 127 finds an equivalent in 282–315, with some highly inspirational modifications. To ensure that the solo line remains idiomatic, more than mere transposition of the second subject is required. As in his keyboard works, Mozart manipulates the melodic contours in bold fashion, especially in his colouring of a modified dialogue between solo registers at bars 303–11, where the introduction of F♯ minor produces an unexpected change of mood. A new counterpoint at bar 303 now has violins playing the melody. For the passage after the pause at bar 315 Mozart reserves his most vivid representation of the imitative passage already heard in bars 25 and 128; it is the clarinet rather than the strings which is now assigned the initial entry. The solo line is then modified in at least two important respects: the alberti figuration accompanying the violin duetting is delayed, so accompanying two bars (324–5) rather than four, whilst the arpeggio figuration at bars 143–4 originally extending over two octaves can now be reconstructed to cover three (bars 331–3), taking advantage of the capabilities of the basset clarinet (Ex. 5, p. 54). Mozart surely calculated this whilst formulating the movement's exposition.

Having displayed a wide variety of virtuoso and idiomatic figures, Mozart proceeds directly to the closing ritornello, passing over the usual opportunity for a true cadenza. He formulates a final orchestral tutti (bars 343–59) from the direct use of bars 16–22 and bars 44–56 in the opening ritornello, thus avoiding any orchestral material which has been subject to solo elaboration during the course of the movement.

Adagio

Whilst outwardly simple in form, the second movement presents a kaleidoscope of innovatory textures, again inspired by the qualities of the solo instrument. The orchestral background is more sombre, influenced in part by the lower tessitura of the horns, reflected in the pre-valve era by their change for this movement to the longer D crooks. The Adagio recalls the mood of the second movement of the Clarinet Quintet, where the tempo is a somewhat faster Larghetto. Mozart's exploitation of the clarinet's upper register develops a type of writing already observed in the concertos of Carl Stamitz, whilst adding a more highly developed operatic dimension. This meeting of music from the theatre with an acute sense of instrumental idiom contributes to the special aura of the whole movement.

The principal theme (bars 1–32) comprises two eight-bar strains, both of which are repeated by the orchestra; each consists of a pair of two-bar phrases with a four-bar continuation. Such an alternation of solo and tutti may also be found within the piano concertos, for example in the Larghetto of the C minor K491. The sheer expressive power of the opening strain of the Adagio of the Clarinet Concerto remains difficult to quantify. Its harmonies are simple, culminating in a straightforward cadence in the dominant A; there is little dissonance, though the melodic line contains a number of expressive intervals. The concealment of Mozart's art is heightened by his combination of operatic melody with a chamber texture, comprising strings alone without double basses. The orchestral response (bars 9–16) is characterised by a change of dynamic to *forte*, an amply scored melodic line and a more active bass line in the lower strings, their former sustaining role transferring to the bassoons. The second solo strain (bars 17–24) maintains an uncomplicated melodic line, though the underlying harmony is increasingly colourful, touching momentarily upon the minor keys of E (bar 19) and F♯ (bar 21). A powerful expressive device is the introduction of some string imitation, filling in alternate bars (18 and 20). On this occasion the orchestral response (bars 25–32) has a more chromatic bass line (see p. 82); different elements in the harmony are highlighted in the winds and the approach to the cadence (bar 31) incorporates a small decoration of the melodic contour.

The middle section (bars 33–59) is entirely solo orientated, introducing a wide variety of rhythms and incorporating a special exploration of the chalumeau register, particularly evident in the reconstruction. Resolutions of cadences on the second beat of the bar contribute to the stylistic continuity throughout the entire passage. The change to a dramatic character is heralded in bars 33–6, with a two-octave downward florid arpeggio countered by an even greater upward leap (bar 35) and some chromatic decoration of the cadence on A (bar 36). Then follows an eight-bar period, constructed (like the movement's main theme) of a pair of two-bar phrases with a four-bar continuation (bars 36–44). Main-beat dissonance in bars 38, 40, 42 and 44 is an important means of expression, with tonality moving back to D (at bars 39–40) and then to an interrupted cadence in A (43–4). The highly distinctive character of the solo writing arises from the variety of rhythms, the chromatic detail and the occurrence of another upward leap of two-and-a-half octaves (bar 41). Then follows an elaboration of the previous eight-bar period, extended to ten (45–54) via leaps and chromatic scales to a cadence in A. The baritone register of the clarinet from bar 45 is matched by some finely calculated orchestral scoring, in which the viola pedal transfers to horns and a pointed figure in first violins lends an exquisite touch of balanced higher tessitura. The *Eingang* at bar 59 is reached via some spectacular arpeggiated figuration (bars 55 and 57), which in the basset version ranges over three octaves.

In the recapitulation, bars 60–75 restate the first two solo strains at bars 1–8 and 17–24, the intervening orchestral response now omitted. Only the cadential approach of bar 23 undergoes a slight melodic alteration at 74. Then follows one of the most original strokes in the entire Concerto: the second orchestral response (bars 25–32) undergoes a significant reharmonisation in bars 76–83, of which the main features are a falling rather than rising bass line in the alternate bars 76, 78 and 80. A vivid reworking in bar 81 replaces relatively plain harmony with a chromatic bass, supporting colourful seventh chords and on the second beat a telling chord of G minor, strangely remote from the next downbeat, an E minor chord.

The coda (from bar 83) introduces to the movement the first occurrence of an anacrusis, whilst drawing together elements of both the principal and middle sections. The intimacy of string accompaniment without double basses recalls the opening, as does the cadence at bar 86, notwithstanding its elaborate and chromatic approach. But the continuation at bars 87–93 recalls the middle section, transforming and extending the material to incorporate the chalumeau register (with its associated sextuplets as upbeat) before approaching the (interrupted) cadence at bars 92–3 via a substantial upward leap and a chromatic run. The final bars have yet more dialogue between the upper register (bars 93–5) and a lower part of the compass (bars 95–8). The orchestral wind, which have been silent throughout the coda, return to add a final touch of colour to the last two bars. The concluding note in the solo part was originally printed as a minim, rather than the crotchet of all the other parts (see Ex. 10a, p. 56); whether this is a subtle, magical effect on the part of Mozart or a simple publisher's misprint has remained a matter for debate.

Rondo: allegro

The third movement contains the complex blend of sonata and rondo forms developed by Mozart within the piano concertos. Its structure, which finds a direct parallel with the rondo of the A major Piano Concerto K488, may be tabulated as follows:

Refrain:	bars 1–56
First episode:	bars 57–113
Refrain:	bars 114–37

Second episode:	bars 137–87
Third episode:	bars 188–246
(recapitulating first episode)	
Refrain:	bars 247–301
Coda:	bars 301–53

As in K488, the refrain is not restated after the second episode, though it does make a final appearance within the coda. Even by comparison with rondos in the piano concertos, a very high proportion of the material throughout the movement is again orientated towards the soloist. This is immediately apparent in the thematic distribution of the refrain. In his piano concertos Mozart had established the framework of a short opening solo statement whose continuation was assigned to the orchestra, whereas in the Clarinet Concerto a far greater degree of dialogue between solo and tutti is evident. The first two bars of the opening theme lie within the interval of a fourth (written e'' $- a''$, sounding $c\#'' - f\#''$), a characteristic shared with the initial solo in the Allegro (bars 1/56–7). Another parallel with the first movement is the light scoring for clarinet, violins and violas. The initial solo statement (bars 1–8) is a model of classical equilibrium, comprising two four-bar complementary phrases. The imperfect cadence at bars 3–4 introduces an immediate chromatic inflection, which is modified to become diatonic at the equivalent point (bar 12) in the orchestral response which follows (bars 9–16). The crescendos at bars 9 and 13 bring the interrupted cadences at bars 10 and 14 into greater focus.

The solo continuation (bars 17–23) comprises scale and arpeggio figuration which appears to be leading to the dominant but in fact prefaces a further statement of the rondo theme (bars 24–31). The codetta to the refrain (31–56) expands the material in dialogue and incorporates some dramatic effects. A rising sequential passage in the violins over a pedal and with sensuous flute and bassoon thirds (bars 31–5) releases a solo response (36–9) closely related to elements of the opening. A further orchestral outburst of just three bars (40–2) provokes some solo virtuosity (43–51), which takes the interrupted cadence at bar 6 as inspiration. In the closing tutti (bars 51–6) the three repeated notes at the head of the principal theme assume significance in the bass line, whilst the repeated notes in the violins and the *forte* dynamic recall the theatricality of the first movement at 1/227.

After a clearly articulated A major cadence, the first episode takes as a starting point a simple figure originally heard in the first violins at bar 46. The initial solo (bars 57–72) introduces idioms tailored to Stadler's instrument, such as the three-octave arpeggio at bar 62. After eight bars the theme recurs in the basset register, cadencing in the dominant at bar 72. E major is eventually established at bar 84 via an exquisite turn to the minor mode, which at bar 77 features a delicate balance of flute solo accompanied by basset clarinet replacing violas in the middle of the string texture. The solo features a high degree of chromaticism at bars 84–97 in the course of further virtuoso writing. In the following cadential dialogue (bars 97–113) between solo (in all registers) and tutti, the pedal point of E is enlivened by the prominent augmented sixths (bars 104, 106, 108, 111).

The refrain which begins at bar 114 dispenses with the initial anacrusis and varies the first bar, but is otherwise an exact restatement, leading to a tutti (bars 121–37) which develops the orchestral material originally heard at bars 51–6. The *forte* dynamic and repeated-note string figuration generate a character which is in marked contrast to the surrounding solo passages. As the music modulates towards F# minor there is effective employment of hemiola rhythm at bars 131–2.

As in the A major Piano Concerto K488, the principal tonalities of the second episode are F# minor and D major. But in contrast to K488, the lyrical material precedes the dramatic. Bars 137–45 present a statement of an eight-bar theme whose slower rhythmic impulse contrasts with other solo material within the rondo. This is answered in the lower register (bars 146–57), as if by another character on the operatic stage; the extension of this version of the theme draws on an accompaniment figure first heard at bar 73. The following passage (bars 158–87) is one of the most dramatic showcases for the basset clarinet in the entire Concerto, featuring spectacular leaps, together with dialogue between soprano and baritone registers. After a D major cadence at bar 178 occurs a development of bar 1 for clarinet and the two violin parts featuring the soloist variously as melodist and bass line, whilst introducing a rare contrapuntal element with an expressiveness heightened by some potent use of dissonance.

Following an imperfect cadence in A, the recapitulatory third episode begins with a conventional restatement (188–95) of bars 57–64. Then follows an especially ingenious passage, which introduces a variety of new perspectives on the original material. At bar 196 comes an abrupt turn to the minor, which directly parallels the equivalent context (bar 320) in the rondo of K488. But instead of a mere restatement in the minor mode, another highly chromatic dialogue passage (bars 196–207) based on bar 188 again has the solo clarinet as both melodist and carrier of the bass line. The material modulates from A minor via C major to D minor for the new passage of sequential solo figuration at bars 208–13, which leads back to A minor. In this tonality bars 214–17 restate the complete phrase of 73–6, played now for the first time by the soloist. This leads to an overtly rhetorical gesture. The first two bars of the main theme of the episode are detached and played by upper strings (bar 218–19) and then by clarinet and lower strings (bars 220–1), each statement separated by a fermata. The continuation from bar 222 has the orchestration of flute solo and clarinet bass line from bars 77ff, with alterations and elisions in the reappearance of the semiquaver figuration from bars 84–7. This episode as a whole represents a miracle of creative reworking of material. At its close the virtuoso cadential passage from bars 88 to 96 is omitted, but then the approach to the refrain at bars 230–46 directly recapitulates bars 97–113.

Apart from the absence of an initial anacrusis, the refrain (bars 247–301) exactly recapitulates bars 1–55. Development of the rondo theme is an important feature of the extended and virtuosic coda (bars 301–53). Its introduction comprises striking arpeggiated patterns (bars 301–6) ranging over the three principal solo registers. The continuing dialogue (bars 307–10) is based on the semiquaver figuration in the very first bar of the rondo, its descent into the chalumeau register followed by three bars (311–13) of low solo accompaniment to the strings, recalling the first movement textures of 1/134–7 and 324–5. Characteristic leaps, trills and scalar figuration lead to a perfect cadence in bar 3/322. There follows a striking dialogue (bars 322–7) between solo and upper strings based on the first bar of the rondo theme, but with the introduction of further chromaticism and expressive dissonance; this derives from the end of the second episode at bar 178. A solo continuation and chromatic lead-in (bars 328–33) presage the final statement of the rondo theme, given an interrogative twist by means of a rising final note (341) and extended by two bars (342–3), at the cadence (bars 344–6) featuring one last display of characteristic leaps. After such an imaginative coda, Mozart ends with a brief theatrical tutti (bars 346–53), based on the orchestral material at bar 121 and recalling the hemiola effect within that passage.

7

Performance practice

Introduction

Is the kind of performance expected by Mozart in his own day valid for later generations of players? We can never really answer this question, if only because so many relevant parameters have changed during the last couple of centuries. For example, the discipline imposed by the microphone and the implications of air travel are two factors which have brought about such changes that we cannot have the option to turn back the clock. Even if we could hear Anton Stadler's première of Mozart's Clarinet Concerto, we would not necessarily wish to adopt all of its features; like all performers of our own day (on modern or period instruments), we should continue to exercise elements of choice and taste as much characteristic of the twentieth century as of the eighteenth. But the mere fact that the original performance conditions can seem at all relevant now marks a radical shift in our musical thinking.

Period performance of Mozart and his contemporaries has recently been subject to reassessment in the light of the evidence of early recordings. As one eminent scholar in the field has succinctly put it, 'If early recordings teach us anything, it is that no musicians can ever escape the taste and judgement of their own time'.[1] Was there ever a time when our clean, accurate approach prevailed, as has recently been asserted in relation to Mozart's symphonies? ' . . . A neo-classical performance . . . cannot have the on-going shaping, the personal interpretation, that we treasure in performances . . . by great modern conductors, nor would it have been practical to create such performances in the single rehearsal usually allotted symphonies in the eighteenth century. . . . The results are bound to be more neutral and less personal, more objective and less subjective.'[2] This comment seems to be all too indicative of a late-twentieth-century dogma of constraint, where our own competence tends to be measured by skill at maintaining executive control at all costs, and personality is all too easily underplayed.

Tempo flexibility

Timing and tempo flexibility are areas where the aesthetic still apparent in early recordings has all but disappeared. The playing of clarinettists (and other instrumentalists) from the first decade of the twentieth century encourages the thought that flexibility of tempo has become almost a lost art. For only in our own times has a self-effacing reading of the score begun to replace an intuitive response to the code contained within the musical notation itself. Of course, there were many admonitions to keep strict time during the eighteenth and nineteenth centuries, because the ability to keep a steady beat was difficult to acquire and a mark of professionalism. C. P. E. Bach and a host of later writers were in fact warning against tempo modification which occurred unintentionally. A generation after Mozart's death, Spohr called for strict observance of time but his requirements for a 'fine style' included increasing the tempo in furious, impetuous passages (anathema to many present-day performers) and slowing up for tender, melancholy moments.[3] Is there evidence for this kind of flexibility in the late eighteenth century?

Relevant to an emphasis on the darker elements in Mozart's Clarinet Concerto are the following remarks by the pianist Daniel Türk, encouraging a greater degree of freedom: 'A tenderly, moving passage between two lively, fiery ideas . . . can be played somewhat hesitatingly; only in this case one does not take the tempo gradually slower, but *immediately* a little (however, only *a little*) slower'.[4] The minor-mode transitions in the first movement at 1/78ff and especially 1/272ff (Ex. 2b, p. 33) and also the opening of the development in the Rondo (3/138ff) might seem particularly appropriate contexts for such treatment. Underlining the whole issue is the fact that we are bound to interpret eighteenth-century evidence from the viewpoint of our own musical taste, which has tended to become less flexible and improvisatory than in earlier times.

The rhetorical style: articulation and nuance

Inevitably, there was much detail which Mozart did not trouble to write into his scores; he simply expected that certain conventions would be observed, especially in relation to articulation and phrasing. Backofen's clarinet tutor states quite simply that a composer cannot indicate how he would like each note played, but must place his trust in the performer's sensibility. No study of performance practice can bridge the vast gap between what is contained in the score and its intended execution. But the detached, articulate style current in Mozart's day has proved to be worth recapturing not merely for historical reasons but also for its musical effect; in classical documents, expressive performance is consistently seen as the result of attention to detail. Modern clarinet playing in many parts of the world has arguably moved further in the direction of a smooth, seamless approach than either the flute or oboe, using a correspondingly narrower range of articulations. It is salutary to note that the flautist Quantz expected a huge range of articulation, assigning great importance to the tongue, by which animation was given to the execution of notes, rather like a violin bow-stroke.

The importance of nuance is an underlying theme throughout the clarinet tutor written by Lefèvre for the Paris Conservatoire in 1802. He remarked that clarinet playing is monotonous when the artist fails to nuance the sound and to penetrate the composer's intentions. Uniformity of execution and articulation means that a coldness and monotony has often been attributed to the nature of the instrument, whereas it belongs rather to the player who cannot take advantage of its capabilities. Türk's study of piano playing develops the analogy of music with speech; the performer must make the music meaningful, just as the orator has it in his power to make either intelligible or ambiguous a sentence such as 'He lost his life not only his fortune'.

To complement intelligibility, communication of emotion in music was regarded as an absolute priority, both Quantz and C. P. E. Bach remarking that if a player was not himself moved by what he played, he would never move others, which should be his real aim. These comments were written well before the nineteenth-century cultivation of virtuosity as an end in itself or the veneration for accuracy brought about by the age of recording. In assuming a good knowledge of harmony and the art of singing, eighteenth-century writers were in fact expecting that the performer would glean a great deal of interpretative information from the rhythm, melodic intervals, phrasing and harmony notated in the score and adapt his technique accordingly.

Ornamentation and improvisation

Türk was much occupied with ornamentation (both notated and improvised), stating that one should be guided by the character of the context. Baroque improvisation was still widely practised, and his first thought was that any additions should suit the prevailing character. Extempore embellishments must be used sparingly and in the right place,

. . . since the art of variation presumes, in addition to a great deal of knowledge of harmony, a very refined taste, good judgement, skill in execution, security in counting &c, only an accomplished master, and only when he is well disposed, should attempt to include ornaments of this kind. . . . Only those places should be varied (but only when the composition is repeated) which would otherwise not be interesting enough and consequently become tedious . . .[5]

In the outer movements of the Clarinet Concerto, very little solo material is in fact repeated. In the first movement the opening of the exposition (1/57–80) recurs (1/251–74), whilst in the Rondo the only thematic material to appear more than once (apart from the main theme itself) is the passage at 3/57–64, which recurs at 3/188–95. We have already noted the potential for elaboration at 1/216–19.

Does Mozart's Adagio invite the addition of ornamentation? In discussing this type of context Türk writes that any elaboration must appear to have been achieved with ease:

There are certain compositions or individual sections which are so communicative and speak so directly to the heart of the listener, without any false glitter, that in such cases a beautiful tone corresponding to the character of the music, played softly or more strongly, are the only means by which the expression should be made more intense.[6]

Caution is also encouraged by Heinrich Koch, who in 1802 remarks: 'we have to ask whether a musical idea, expressed in noble simplicity, needs embellishment and whether it would not be advantageous to try to execute it in its elevated simplicity rather than smudge it with idle glitter'.[7] But a powerful counter-argument is provided by a surviving elaboration of K488(ii) reproduced in facsimile and transcription in *NMA Kritischer Bericht* V/15/7. Recently identified as the work of Mozart's pupil Barbara Ployer, its very boldness is instructive, whether or not the detail was explicitly approved (or suggested) by the composer. To support a case that (at any rate) the second strain of the recapitulation at bars 2/68–75 of K622 be embellished (for example, as at Ex. 14), we might note that Mozart himself reharmonizes the tutti which follows.

Cadenzas

The lack of opportunity for a true cadenza represents an important departure within Mozart's concertos. As already noted in the preceding analysis, the fermatas at bars 1/127 and 1/315 call merely for modest cadential ornamentation rather than an extended improvisation, whilst bar 59 of the Adagio

Ex. 14

presents a similar case. In these three contexts a fermata over or after a dominant-seventh chord precedes the return of a theme or a larger formal section.

For the Adagio of the Concerto, performances have traditionally borrowed the equivalent passage at bars 2/49–50 of the Clarinet Quintet. This may have been the so-called 'sorry affair' played by Willman in 1838, in which case its very context was probably misunderstood by the critic of the *Musical World* (22 March 1838, p. 199). More extended interpolations by succeeding clarinettists and scholars have tended to reflect the musical taste of their own time rather than that of Mozart. For example, the virtuoso Carl Baermann furnished his 1870 edition with a cadenza, which, though relatively modest in length, contrives a reference to bar 108 of the first movement before anticipating the principal theme of the Adagio which follows.[8]

Ferruccio Busoni's 1922 Breitkopf and Härtel edition of the Adagio interpolated a twenty-bar accompanied cadenza, characterised by intensely chromatic harmonies and prominent anticipation of the movement's coda. Busoni also composed cadenzas for nine of Mozart's piano concertos and for the slow movements of the flute concertos, whose freedom of form, texture and harmonic language reflect his own highly individual personality in an era when strict adherence to an earlier composer's style was not regarded as a priority.[9]

A set of three cadenzas was provided by the distinguished Czech clarinettist Stanislav Krticka (1887–1969) in his 1939 tutor for the Müller- and Boehm-system clarinets, *Skola pro normální a francouzsky klarinet*. Significantly, their title in the first edition was 'Three cadenzas in B-flat for the Concerto for B-flat clarinet by W. A. Mozart', indicating that this was the instrument on which the piece was at that time likely to be studied, if not performed. For the Adagio Krticka provided an improvisatory elaboration of the dominant seventh, whose flights of fancy encompass references to 1/108 and 2/33 and 2/55, as well as anticipation of the principal theme. For the first-movement fermatas he contrives a matching pair of fifteen-bar elaborations incorporating some far-flung chromatic figuration. It is again the function as much as the style of these cadenzas which modern taste will want to call into question.[10]

In 1950 Jacques Ibert composed two virtuoso cadenzas for a new edition for Leduc by Ulysse Delécluse, which was published the following year.[11] Ibert left bar 1/127 unadorned, perhaps because of the uninviting bar's rest in the solo part, following the fermata. Bar 1/315 is of course closer to the point in the first movement where a cadenza might normally be expected, and Mozart's cadence inspires thirty-two bars of wide-ranging declamation. Rugged chromatic contours combine with great rhythmic variety, virtuoso leaps and the use of repeated notes as an expressive device. The interpolation also features a somewhat curious insistence on a high f'''. Ibert's cadenza for the Adagio is shorter and more focused tonally, though its inclusion of an anacrusis towards the end weakens the structural effect of Mozart's coda to the movement. Though more modest in scope than Busoni's cadenza, its roulades scarcely complement the character of Mozart's surrounding material.[12]

The cadenzas by Karlheinz Stockhausen date from 1978 and were published in 1985. His elaboration of bar 1/127 is brief and conventional, referring to the second half of the movement's opening bar. Bar 1/315 is extended to a total of six bars, with an elaboration of the dominant-seventh chord featuring the trill figure first heard in bars 39ff of the orchestral ritornello. Stockhausen's interpolation is marked *forte* and climaxes on a held f''' in his third bar. At 2/59 he adds seven bars, marked *langsamer als Adagio* and featuring slow leaps between e or f and bb'' or b''. The passage features carefully calculated dynamic contrasts and changes of colour, the latter indicated by instructions for vibrato and the inclusion of sets of fingerings for the production of b'' and c''' as unaccustomed harmonics.

For all the imagination exhibited by later composers, current concern for Mozart's own intentions is likely to prefer either to continue to borrow material from the Adagio of his Quintet, or perhaps to construct a lead-in analogous with the extant *Eingänge* for basset clarinet intended for insertion in the Michl Concerto and discussed in Chapter 3. A possible solution of this type might be the suggestion in Example 15.

The soloist as director

It may be assumed that Stadler, having arrived in Prague with Mozart's score, proceeded to direct the performance, with some assistance from the Konzertmeister. It seems possible that as part of the directorial operation

Ex. 15

Stadler may have played at the very opening of the work (perhaps for eight bars or so), in the concluding bars of the first movement, and at the very end of the work. Conversely, solo participation in the Adagio tuttis would clearly detract from the dialogue which lies at its very heart. Indeed, one of the distinguishing features of a classical clarinet concerto is that solo involvement in tuttis has a far greater influence on tone-colour than is the case with concertos for such instruments as the violin or bassoon. The unidiomatic solo part traditionally notated in the tuttis has no bearing on the issue, being a mere cueing device inserted by the publisher. A similar convention may be observed within the first edition of Mozart's G major Flute Concerto K313/258c published by Breitkopf and Härtel in 1803, where as early as bar 10 in the first tutti the soloist is apparently required to produce the note *b*, a semitone below the flute's actual compass.[13]

Other matters relating to original performance conditions include the possibility that string forces may well have been reduced during solo passages, for which there is some evidence from other eighteenth-century concerto material.[14] A more controversial issue remains the continued participation of a keyboard player in Viennese instrumental repertoire of this period.[15] With the possible exception of 2/36 (where Mozart links the solo phrases with a mere bass line), the Concerto offers little suggestion that a fortepiano might contribute usefully to the texture. Like so many of the issues addressed during the course of this book, such a question might well be answered by the recovery of Mozart's autograph score. Even two hundred years after the disappearance of such a precious manuscript, it would be premature to regard this loss as irrevocable.

Appendix 1

A review of the Breitkopf and Härtel edition in the Leipzig Allgemeine Musikalische Zeitung, 4 *(March 1802), columns 408-13*

The original musical examples are included here. In a number of places the author simply cites the page numbers and lines of the clarinet part under review. To these references have been added bar numbers in square brackets. The following translation by William McColl originally appeared in *The Clarinet*, 9/2 (1982), and is reproduced with his kind permission.

Review

Concert pour Clarinette avec accompagnement de 2 Violons, 2 Flûtes, 2 Bassons, 2 Cors, Viola (Alto) et Basse par W. A. Mozart. Chez Breitkopf *et* Härtel, *à Leipsic* (Price 2 Thalers)

The reviewer, who has this magnificent concerto lying before him in score form, can impart to all *good* clarinettists the happy certainty that none other than *Mozart* – only *he* – can have written it; that consequently it must be, in view of the beautiful, proper, and tasteful composition, the foremost clarinet concerto in the world; for, so far as the reviewer knows, only this one by him exists. Of course it is difficult, and even *very* difficult, whereof anyone even partially familiar with the clarinet will be easily convinced by the most fleeting perusal of a few places in this concerto; for example, right on the first page, line thirteen and following [1/79-83]. But what clarinettist would not gladly subject himself to the pleasant effort and pastime of studying it, practising it and learning it *well*, as he will then – and must – secure the finest reward for an artist as artist, namely, to delight and enrapture himself and all around him by the omnipotence of true art? Truly the reviewer remains firmly *convinced* that good execution of *this* concerto will bestow honour and admiration upon *every* able clarinettist as it will bestow pleasure upon every listener, *whatever* his sensibilities and *whichever* type of music he may love most, if only he has *feeling* for this heavenly art. The first allegro is splendidly crafted and contains almost all of those phrases and coloraturas whereby the *skilful* clarinettist can shine outstandingly. The *emotional* man will find in the adagio more than he needs to communicate and generally to awaken the deepest feeling. Should, however, anyone have neither the knowledge to admire the first movement, nor feeling for the second, he will still, one hopes, be sufficiently *amused* by the wit and humour, as fine as it is noble, of the third movement, a very pleasing rondo. However, if this, too, leaves him cold and unsatisfied; if he feels nothing at all in it whereby the consciousness of some inner pleasure or comfort, some gratification or charm might deepen its mystery or explain itself; then he can take this for the surest and most infallible sign or symptom that for *this* art he has neither sense nor feeling.

Repeatedly the reviewer has felt sorry, when judging *outstandingly good* works, not to be able to make apparent to his readers even the *pre-eminent* beauties or perfections therein without writing down a considerable part of the whole, for which even the most extended limits of these notices would be inadequate by far: whereas, on the contrary, it is so easy, and requires so little to look for, write down, and make evident blots and errors of all kinds, large and small. Thus also in this concerto lying before us there are infinitely many details which, looked at *individually* for themselves alone, are admittedly quite proper and cute, but *as such* they are still only details, all of which, however, conjoined as well-ordered parts of the whole, raise it to what it really is – a *masterpiece*. Although I cannot give eyewitness *proof* of this claim and of that made at the beginning of this review [that the concerto is by Mozart], to *connoisseurs* and worshippers of Mozart's compositions it will be sufficient to quote only the beginning theme and a few canonic alterations in double counterpoint derived therefrom, all of which appear already in the first ritornello, as well as a small part of the incomparably beautiful adagio, which transports one to a tender melancholy.

In order to save as much space as possible the reviewer has printed the main voices in these examples on only *two* staves. What extraordinary effects Mozart could achieve through the most precise knowledge of all the customary instruments and their most advantageous employment; that especially *in this respect* Mozart has been equalled by *nobody*: this *everyone* knows, and will therefore, I hope, give due consideration to it regarding these examples.

Theme:

Canonic alteration in double counterpoint at the duodecimo, &c [1/25]:
Imitations in double counterpoint at the octave and tenth [1/31]:

From the Adagio, 3/4 time in D major:

Lastly, the reviewer finds it necessary to remark that Mozart wrote this concerto for a clarinet which goes down to C. Thus, for example, all the following places in the solo part must be transposed an octave lower: Page 4, system 10, bars 1 and 2, the first crotchet [of each of bars 1/146 and 147]. Page 5, system 3, bar 6 from the second crotchet until system 4, bar 7, the third crotchet [bars 1/190–8]. Page 5, system 5, the last three notes [bar 1/206 and the first half of 1/207]. Page 5, system 6, in the second bar the last two notes, and the first note of the third bar [bars 1/208 and 209].

Page 3, system 15, bar 2 [i.e. 1/94],

instead of

should be:

And page 4, system 10, bar 3 [1/148],

instead of

should be:

And in *this* way, *very many* places have been transposed and changed. This is especially striking in the adagio, page 7, system 5, bars 6 and 7 [2/45 and 46]; system 6, bars 1–5 [2/47–51]; and system 7, bar 3 [2/55], etc.

Above all, however, the transposition in the rondo, page 8, system 8, the second half of the first bar and the first half of the second bar [bars 3/61 and 62], as also on page 9 the last two bars and on page 10 the first two bars [probably 3/99 to the first half of 105], etc.

Whereas nowadays such clarinets descending to low C must still be counted among the rare instruments, one is indebted to the editors for these transpositions and alterations for the normal clarinet, although the concerto has not exactly gained thereby. Perhaps it would have been just as well to have published it entirely according to its original version and to have rendered these transpositions and alterations at most by smaller notes.

Music Director Müller in Leipzig has transposed this concerto into G major from A major, arranged it for the flute, and this is the same concerto which has appeared under the following title:

Concert pour la Flûte traversière avec accompagnement de 2 Violons, 2 Hautbois, 2 Cors, 2 Bassons, Viola (Alto) et Basse, par W. A. Mozart, arrangé d'un Concert pour Clarinette p. A. E. Müller. Chez Breitkopf et Härtel à Leipzic. (Price two Thalers).

Whereas one sooner encounters twenty mediocre flautists than one finds even *one* bearable clarinettist, Mr Müller deserves credit for the usefulness of his excellent work.

However much this concerto stands out to its advantage when compared to even the more excellent flute concertos; moreover, unmistakable as is the care which Mr Müller has devoted to this arrangement, it profits neither by the transposition to the lower key of G nor much less by the very numerous, however absolutely necessary, alterations and rewritings. Furthermore, if – at least in the reviewer's opinion – the flute must yield to the clarinet by a wide margin as an instrument suitable for concertos, then this arrangement can especially please only those who lack the opportunity to become acquainted with the concerto in its original form. On the other hand, as there is by no means a surplus of really good flute concertos, these sorts of phenomena must at least be very pleasing to good flautists.

Appendix 2

Surviving instruments

A list of clarinets and basset horns relevant in design and provenance to the study of Mozart's Clarinet Concerto, compiled for this appendix by Nicholas Shackleton.

[Y] numbers refer to Phillip T. Young, *4900 Historical Woodwind Instruments: An Inventory of 200 makers in International Collections* (London, 1993); see also makers' entries in William Waterhouse, *The New Langwill Index: A Dictionary of Musical Wind-Instrument Makers and Inventors* (London, 1993).

1 Basset clarinets

Basset clarinets were first made during the late eighteenth century to a variety of designs, pitched in the keys of B♭, A and C. Their distinguishing feature from normal clarinets is the addition of lower notes below the usual written bottom note *e*, as on basset horns of the period. Table 1 lists clarinets that by any stretch might be called basset clarinets. The first three probably date from the 1770s, and illustrate the fact that extended clarinets existed before Stadler's time. No. 1 is sickle-shaped like the basset horns by the same maker. Nos. 2 and 3 are a pair with curved brass crooks and straight bodies. These three descend to low *c* but without the intervening *d*. No. 4 is curved but unlike No. 1 the body is made of curved pieces of boxwood joined together, each piece being cylindrically bored; this method would be capable of making a more precise bore than the method used to make No. 1. This instrument is in effect a five-keyed clarinet with a diatonic basset extension; that is to say it has the minimum keywork of the classical clarinet, with an additional low *d* and *c*. Nos. 5, 6, 7, 8 and 9 have varying numbers of additional keys such as were commonly being added by many of the better makers during the first quarter of the nineteenth century. No. 6 is built like many Viennese basset horns, with the extension contained in a thrice-bored *Buch*. This instrument has suitable keywork for the Mozart Concerto except that the basset extension is diatonic.

Table 1

1	Mayrhofer	Y3	D-Passau: Oberhausmuseum: in A
2	anon. AS		F-Paris: Conservatoire: in A
3	anon. AS		F-Paris: Conservatoire: in A
4	anon.		D-Berlin: in A
5	Strobach		D-Hamburg: in A
6	anon. (German)		F-Paris: Conservatoire: in A
7	Eisenbrandt		on loan to NL-Hoeprich: in C (illustrated in Fig. 4.1)
8	Larshoff		CH-Zumikon: Stalder: in A
9	Bischoff		D-Darmstadt: in B♭
10	anon.		GB-Oxford: Bate: in B♭

2 Clarinets

Table 2 lists clarinets of clear Viennese origin. Virtually all are from after Mozart's death, but in general these instruments have a character that is distinctly different from that of contemporary instruments from other parts of Europe. This is due to a combination of larger tone-holes (especially at the bottom of the instrument) and generous undercutting of the tone-holes. They were used with an exceptionally narrow mouthpiece.

Table 2

			(i) in A
1	anon.		A-Graz Joanneum: KGW 1.394
2	Griesbacher	Y1	D-Leipzig: 1484 (pre-1800)
3	Tauber	Y1	GB-Cambridge: Shackleton
4	Merklein		A-Vienna: KM 328[1]
5	Merklein		GB-Cambridge: Shackleton
6	Griesbacher	Y4	CS-Prague: Nat. Mus. 1673E

Table 2 (*cont.*)

(ii) in B♭

1	Lotz	Y1	CH-Geneva: Musée Instr. 136
2	Doleisch	Y2[2]	GB-Cambridge: Shackleton (dated 1793)
3	Bauer[3]	Y1	GB-Cambridge: Shackleton (dated 1789)
4	Hammig		A-Graz: Diözesanmuseum DM 9 (dated 1798)
5	Griesbacher	Y7	A-Salzburg: Mozarthaus, pre-1800[4]
6	Griesbacher	Y3	I-Bergamo: Museo
7	Griesbacher	Y5	D-Frankfurt/Oder: Mus. Viadriana 185
8	Tauber	Y3	GB-Cambridge: Shackleton
9	Tauber	Y7	D-Zell: Hailperin
10	Doleisch	Y3	CS-Prague: Nat. Mus. 1017E (dated 1802)
11	Wolrath		A-Graz: Joanneum KGW 1.393

3 Basset horns

Table 3 lists the basset horns made by major makers in the Vienna–Prague region around Mozart's time. Lotz and Griesbacher were directly associated with Mozart; Merklein and Hammig made basset horns in a similar style. The instruments made by Doleisch are of a somewhat different style but are listed because of Mozart's association with Prague. Two instruments by Strobach are listed because their form with the globular bell is now associated with Stadler's basset clarinet. Of the few identified basset horns in G, Nos. 1 and 2 are certainly earlier than the Concerto; the date of No. 3 (which resembles the instruments by Strobach) may be around 1800; the basset extension is diatonic.

Table 3

(i) in F

1	Lotz	Y1	D-Berlin: 2911[5]
2	Lotz	Y2	CS-Prague: 1365E
3	Lotz	Y3	D-Konstanz: Rosgarten Mus. J19
4	Lotz	Y4	CS-Prague[5]
5	Lotz	Y5	D-Nuremberg: GNM MI 135

Table 3 (*cont.*)

6	Griesbacher	Y1	NL-Amsterdam: Hoeprich
7	Griesbacher	Y2	GB-Cambridge: Shackleton
8	Griesbacher	Y3	GB-London: RCM 242
9	Griesbacher	Y4	USA-MA-Boston: MFA 17.1882
10	Griesbacher	Y5	GB-Cambridge: Shackleton
11	Griesbacher	Y6	I-Modena: Museo 33-1981
12	Hammig		F-Paris: Buffet-Crampon
13	Merklein 1[6]		A-Vienna: KM 340
14	Merklein 2		D-Halle: Handelhaus MS 408
15	Strobach 1		GB-Edinburgh: EUCHMI 969
16	Strobach 2		D-Munich: DM 63678
17	anon. (Doleisch Y4)		D-Halle: Handelhaus MS 406
18	Doleisch	Y1	CS-Prague: Nat. Mus. 467E (dated 1791)
19	Doleisch	Y2	CS-Prague: Nat. Mus. 464E (dated 1793)
20	Doleisch	Y3	USA-SD-Vermillion: Shrine 3541 (dated 1793)
21	Doleisch	Y5	CS-Prague: Hlavni Museum
22	anon. (Doleisch Y6)		CS-Prague: Nat. Mus. 476E
23	Doleisch	Y7	CS-Prague: Nat. Mus. 466E (dated 1796)
24	Doleisch	Y8	B-Brussels: Conservatoire 938 (dated 1797)
25	Doleisch	Y9	GB-London: RCM 90 (dated 1803)

(ii) in G

1	Mayrhofer[7]	Y1	D-Nuremberg: GNM MI 133
2	Mayrhofer	Y2	D-Bonn: Beethovenhaus 154
3	anon.[8]		D-Munich: DM 50897

The following illustration references and detailed descriptions of the basset clarinets in Table 1 have been supplied by Albert Rice:

1. Anton and Michael Mayrhofer, Passau (*fl.* second half of eighteenth century). Curved or sickle-shaped octagonal body covered in brown leather. A rectangular-shaped box section is attached to the lower end of

the body and a metal bell is attached to the end of this section. The box includes a bore which angles once at about 75° before leading directly into the bell. Mouthpiece and barrel are missing. Seven brass keys: register, a', $a\flat/e\flat''$, f/c'', $f\sharp/c\sharp''$, e/b' and c. Passau, Oberhausmuseum, no. 3160 (formerly Hamburg, Museum für Hamburgische Geschichte, 1727.159). Illustrated in Anthony Baines, *European and American Musical Instruments* (London, 1966), no. 641. Also illustrated in Hans Schröder, *Verzeichnis der Sammlung alter Musikinstrumente* (Hamburg, 1930), Abb. 20a (but incorrectly assembled); the same photograph is found in Oskar Kroll, *The Clarinet* (Eng. trans. London, 1968), pl. 15, and F. Geoffrey Rendall, *The Clarinet* (3rd edn, London, 1971), pl. 6a.

2. AS. Three sections of fruitwood, a curved metal neck and an ebony mouthpiece. Seven brass keys: register, a', $a\flat/e\flat''$ (two on either side of the f/c'' key), f/c'', e/b' and c. Paris, Musée de la Musique, E.190 C543. Illustrated in *Instruments de musique 1750-1850* (Paris, 1982), p. 63.

3. AS. Another instrument of the same specifications. Illustrated as (2) above. Paris, Musée de la Musique, E. 2194. This pair of instruments has been sometime attributed to Antoni Schintler; their pitch has been variously identified as A, A♭ or G.

4. Anonymous (missing a *corps de rechange* for tuning to B♭). Four sections of boxwood with ivory ferrules constructed in a curved form, boxwood mouthpiece. Eight brass keys: register, a', $a\flat/e\flat''$, f/c'', $f\sharp/c\sharp''$, e/b', d and c. Berlin, Musikinstrumenten Museum, no. 2886. Illustrated in Curt Sachs, *Sammlung alter Musikinstrumente bei der Staatlichen Hochschule für Musik zu Berlin: beschreibender Katalog* (Berlin, 1922), Tafel 29; and Jean Jeltsch, 'La clarinette de Mozart', *Crescendo: Le Magazine de la musique ancienne*, no. 34 (July–August 1990), p. 17.

5. Strobach, Carlsbad (*fl.* early nineteenth century). Six sections of box-wood with ivory ferrules, the left-hand section angled towards the player at about 60°. A small L-shaped section angled at about 115° connects the right-hand section to a globular-shaped bell. Thirteen brass keys: register, a' to b' trill key, a', $g\sharp'$, $e\flat'/b\flat''$, $c\sharp'/g\sharp''$, $b/f\sharp''$, $b\flat/f''$, $a\flat/e\flat''$, $f\sharp/c\sharp''$, e/b', d and c. Hamburg, Museum für Kunst und Gewerbe, 1912.1562. Illustrated in Hans Schröder, *Verzeichnis der Sammlung alter Musikinstrumente*

(Hamburg, 1930), Abb. 20g; Oskar Kroll, *The Clarinet* (London, 1968), pl. 15; F. Geoffrey Rendall, *The Clarinet* (3rd edn, London, 1971), pl. 6g; Jean Jeltsch, 'La clarinette de Mozart', *Crescendo: Le Magazine de la musique ancienne*, no. 34 (July–August 1990), p. 18.

6. Anonymous. Four sections of stained boxwood without ferrules, and with curved barrel. The left-hand section is angled towards the player at about 40°. A box section with three windways is attached at the lower end of the right-hand section (made in the same manner as the basset horn). Mouthpiece, barrel and metal bell are modern replacements. Nine brass keys: register, *a'*, *eb'/bb'''*, *c#'/g#'''*, *b/f#''*, *f#/c#''*, *e/b'*, *d* and *c*. Paris, Musée de la Musique, 2646 980.2.566.

7. Johann Benjamin Eisenbrandt, Göttingen (*fl.* 1785–1822). Five sections of boxwood with ivory ferrules, includes a curved ivory barrel, and a blackwood mouthpiece. A bulbous bell (with the outer end blocked off by a cap and a large hole bored in the upper side) is attached at the lower end of the instrument by a small L-shaped section angled at 90°. Eleven brass keys: register, *a'* to *b'* trill key, *a'*, *ab/eb''*, *f#/c#''*, *e/b'*, *eb*, *d*, *db* and *c*, plus one with unknown function.

8. Jacob Georg Larshoff, Copenhagen (*fl.* 1798–1834). Four sections of boxwood with ivory ferrules and a darkwood mouthpiece. Fourteen brass keys: register, *a'* to *b'* trill key, *a'*, *g#'*, *f'/c'''* (probably a later addition), *eb'/bb''* (probably a later addition), *c#'/g#''*, *b/f#''* (probably a later addition), *bb/f''*, *ab/eb''*, *f#/c#''*, *e/b'*, *d* and *c*. A second stock section includes keys for *ab/eb''*, *f#/c#''*, *e/b'* to play as a normal clarinet.

9. Johann Gottlieb Karl Bischoff, Darmstadt (*fl.* 1813–70). Four sections of boxwood with ivory ferrules and an ivory mouthpiece. Fifteen brass keys: register, *a'* to *b'* trill key, *a'*, *g#'*, *f'/c'''*, *eb'/bb''*, *c#'/g#''*, *b/f#''*, *bb/f''*, *ab/eb''*, *f#/c#''*, *eb*, *d*, *db* and *c*. Darmstadt, Hessisches Landesmuseum, Kg 61: 116. Photographed in frontal view in *Musikinstrumente aus dem Hessischen Landesmuseum 16.-19. Jahrhundert* (Darmstadt, 1980), p. 51; in dorsal view in Jean Jeltsch, 'La clarinette de Mozart', *Crescendo: Le Magazine de la musique ancienne*, no. 34 (July–August 1990), p. 18.

10. Anonymous, Paris (late nineteenth century). Four sections of cocus wood with German silver ferrules and a darkwood mouthpiece. Sixteen keys (simple-system keywork with two rings for the right hand): register, a' to b' trill key, a', g', f'/c''', eb'/bb'', $c\#'/g\#''$, ab/eb'', f/c'' (two), $f\#/c\#''$ (two), e/b' (two), d and c. Oxford, Bate Collection, x48. Illustrated in Pamela Poulin, 'The basset clarinet of Anton Stadler', *College Music Symposium*, 22/2 (1982), p. 82; and Colin Lawson, 'The basset clarinet revived', *Early Music*, 15 (1987), p. 499.

Appendix 3

A list of works composed by Mozart's clarinettist, Anton Stadler

Anton Stadler was the earliest composer to publish works for the clarinet alone. Some of his solo material was probably originally intended for basset clarinet, though not published in this form. It seems from concert programmes that Stadler was also the composer of a clarinet concerto, now lost. He also wrote for two clarinets, the basset horn, a sextet of wind instruments (*Harmonie*) and for the Czakan, a duct flute pitched in A or A♭ popular in Vienna around the beginning of the nineteenth century. The following list, together with details of modern editions, has been compiled by Albert Rice.

Clarinet

Trois Caprices pour la Clarinette seule (Vienna: Au Magasin de l'imprimerie chimique [1808]). Vienna: Gesellschaft der Musikfreunde in Wien, VIII 2503; Budapest: Orszegys Széchény Könyvtár. Modern edition, F. G. Höly (Lottstetten/Waldshut: Kunzelmann, 1992)

Trois Fantaisies ou Potpourris pour la Clarinette seule (Vienna: Jean Traeg, *c.* 1809). Budapest: Bartók Béla Zeneművészeti Szakiskola Konyvyára, 70351

Variations sur différents Themas favorits pour la clarinette seule (Vienna: Jean Cappi, *c.* 1810). Melk: Musikarchiv Stift Melk, V 1387. Incomplete modern edition, F. G. Höly (Lottstetten/Waldshut: Kunzelmann, 1990)

Two clarinets

Six Duettinos progressives pour 2 Clarinettes (Vienna: Magasin de l'imprimerie chimique, *c.* 1808). Berlin: Deutsche Staatsbibliothek, 268692

Six Duettinos concertantes pour 2 Clarinettes (Vienna: Haslinger). Modern editions, J. Michaels (Hamburg: Sikorski, 1967) and D. Klöcker (Vienna: Universal, 1986)

Basset horn

'18 Terzetten für 3 Bassetthörner' (MS) Vienna: Gesellschaft der Musikfreunde in Wien, VIII 1227

Czakan

6 Duettinos pour 2 Csákans ou csákan et Violon, nos. 1 and 2 (Vienna: Magazin, 1808). Zagreb: Hrvatski Glazbeni Zavod, 59 4002; Brünn: Mährisches Museum, Dacice, 29433/A 22070. Modern edition for two flutes, H. Prohle (Budapest: Editio Musica, 1981)

7 Variations pour Csákan (Vienna, *c.* 1812). Martin: Matica Slovenska Uhrovec/Zay D, 1/237. Modern edition for recorder, H. Reyne (Wilhelmshaven: Heinrichshofen, 1990)

7 Variations pour Csákan (Vienna, *c.* 1812). Vienna: Stadt- und Landesbibliothek, M 6631/c

Lost compositions

12 ländlerische Tänze für 2 Clarinettes (Vienna: Cappi)

10 Variationen über 'Müsst ma nix in übel aufnehma' für Clarinette (Vienna: J. Traeg, [1810])

9 Variations über 'Müsst ma nix in übel aufnehma' für Csákan (Vienna: J. Traeg, [1810]) [This may have been a work of the same title by Johann Kaiser]

3 Caprices pour Csákan ou Flûte double (Vienna, chem. Druck, *c.* 1811)

2 Märsche [wind sextet] (Vienna: Steiner)

12 deutsche Tänze mit Trios [wind sextet] (Vienna: Steiner)

Notes

Preface

1 *Allgemeine Musikalische Zeitung*, 4 (March 1802), cols. 408–13.
2 For example, Rice, *The Baroque Clarinet*.
3 The *NMA* version for normal clarinet is not quite what its title (*Traditionelle Fassung für Klarinette*) implies; for example, it has an octave downward transposition of parts of bars 1/146 and 147, a feeble effect after the *e′′′* which occurs in the traditional version of 1/145.
4 Including the version prepared for the Breitkopf and Härtel *Mozart-Ausgabe* (1881) by Ernst Rudorff; the Eulenburg Score (1938) by Rudolf Gerber; and more recent editions by Jack Brymer, Klaus Burmeister, Ulysse Delécluse, Alan Hacker, Reginald Kell, Eric Simon, Frederick Thurston and the Trio di Clarone, amongst others.

1 The eighteenth-century clarinet and its music

1 Nickel, *Die Holzblasinstrumentenbau in der freien Reichsstadt Nürnberg*, p. 214.
2 An incomplete three-keyed clarinet in Berkeley has been ascribed with reasonable certainty to J. C. Denner, and this may be the earliest clarinet in existence.
3 Rice, *The Baroque Clarinet*, p. 15.
4 Nickel, *Die Holzblasinstrumentenbau*, pp. 203–5.
5 See Lawson, *The Chalumeau in Eighteenth-Century Music*.
6 Lawson, 'The chalumeau in the works of Fux', in *Johann Joseph Fux and the Music of the Austro-Hungarian Baroque*, ed. H. White (Aldershot, 1992), pp. 78–94.
7 An even later mention of the chalumeau occurs in J. V. Reynvaan's *Musijkaal Kunst-Woordenboek* (Amsterdam, 1795).
8 Schmid, 'Gluck–Starzer–Mozart', pp. 1198–209.
9 Rice, *The Baroque Clarinet*, pp. 162–4.
10 Badische Landesbibliothek, MSS 302, 304, 328, 332, 334 and 337. Heinz Becker, who edited four of the works in *Das Erbe Deutsche Musik* (Wiesbaden, 1957), believed that these concertos were written about 1745 during Molter's second Karlsruhe period as Kapellmeister for the court of Baden-Durlach (1742–65). This volume also contains the two concertos by Franz Pokorný.
11 *The Baroque Clarinet*, p. 110.
12 *Ibid.*, Ex. 4.32, p. 123 and Exx. 4.30 and 4.33, pp. 119–20 and 126–7.
13 Many works of that period and the succeeding years contained directions to the effect that oboes might be replaced by clarinets or vice versa. The *Allgemeine Musikalische Zeitung*, 4 (1802), col. 475, writes about this custom: 'In France (where people tend to go to extremes) the clarinet, instead of the oboe, is in almost general use for symphonies', and Backofen also reports: 'Among the wind instruments, the clarinet is still the favourite of the French and that to such a degree that in symphonies and concertos where the clarinet is not expressly specified, they make it take over the oboe parts'. See Kroll, *The Clarinet*, pp. 48–9.
14 Rice, *The Baroque Clarinet*, pp. 133, 154–5.
15 The quartet is reproduced complete by Rice, *ibid.*, pp. 129–32.

16 Eric Halfpenny, 'Castilon on the clarinet', *Music and Letters*, 35 (1954), p. 338. Castilon describes a four-keyed clarinet, the latest addition a key for *f♯/c♯'''*, rather than that for *a♭/e♭''* which appeared first in Germany.

17 David Charlton, *Orchestration and Orchestral Practice in Paris, 1789 to 1810*, diss. (Cambridge University, 1973), notes that during this period in France the choice of clarinet tended to be the responsibility of the player, a practice later criticised by Berlioz. The large number of scores with C clarinet therefore exaggerates the extent of its actual orchestral usage.

18 Ancelet, *Observations sur la musique, les musiciens, et les instruments* (Amsterdam, 1757), quoted by Rice, *The Baroque Clarinet*, p. 133.

19 Gradenwitz, 'The beginnings of clarinet literature'. The title page specifies scoring with a pair of horns as well as strings, but the wind parts do not survive.

20 These are arrangements from a series of five lost *symphonies concertantes* for oboe and bassoon, published in 1781.

21 Work-list by Fritz Kaiser in *The New Grove Dictionary of Music and Musicians*, ed. S. Sadie (London, 1980), 18, p. 65.

22 Weston, *Clarinet Virtuosi of the Past*, p. 31.

23 *Neues historisch-biographisches Lexicon der Tonkünstler*, II, p. 328.

24 Weston, *Clarinet Virtuosi of the Past*, p. 43.

25 See for example Rice, *The Baroque Clarinet*, pp. 151–6.

26 C. F. Pohl, *Mozart und Haydn in London* (Vienna, 1867/R1970), I, pp. 64, 71–2; II, p. 373.

27 Cited by Weston, *Clarinet Virtuosi of the Past*, p. 26.

28 *Ibid.*, p. 251.

29 Mahon's tutor, which probably dates from *c.* 1803, features the chalumeau register in didactic material, cadenzas and duets. His fingering chart for five-keyed clarinet gives a range to *a'''*, and his table of transpositions shows acquaintance with clarinets in A, B♭, B, C and D, the last 'good for noisy music'. See Andrew Lyle, 'John Mahon's clarinet preceptor', *Galpin Society Journal*, 30 (1977), pp. 52–5.

2 Mozart, Stadler and the clarinet

1 Kroll, *The Clarinet*, p. 59.

2 Birsak, 'Salzburg, Mozart und die Klarinette', pp. 40–7.

3 '2 Clarinetten mit Gänzhals und H Federn auch mit 2 mittern Stück D: und C: Thon.'

4 'Clarinetten mit Riemen & Futteral.' See Oskar Seefeldner, *Das Salzburger Kriegswesen*, Salzburger Museum Carolino Augusteum, HS 4045.

5 Clarinet in D by G. Walch, Berchtesgaden in the Museum Carolino Augusteum, Salzburg, No. 18/2. Constructed of pearwood, the instrument is in three sections and has three brass keys (the third for the thumb) and two bottom holes, enabling it to be played with either hand above the other.

6 Members of the Berchtesgaden family Walch made clarinets in B♭, A, A♭ and G, which are distinguished from the high-pitched instruments by a slightly curved brass crook inserted between the mouthpiece and the upper joint.

7 Completed on 4 July, this quintet in E♭ is scored for clarinet, horn, bassoon, violin and viola, and has been published in a modern edition by G. Balassa (Budapest, 1960). A later Divertimento in C (*c.* 1795) is scored for two basset horns, two horns and two bassoons.

8 Ernst Hintermaier, *Die Salzburger Hofkapelle von 1700–1806*, (diss., Salzburg, 1972), p. XX, pp. 322, 539.

9 *Divertimento, Salzburg 22 July bis 4 August 1764, 2 Fl/ 2 Ob/ Clarinet (concertato)/ 2 Fg/ 2 H/ 2 Clarini/ Trombone (concertato) / 2 V/ 2 V/ 2 Vcl/ Bass.* Autograph, Budapest, Nationalbibliothek, MS Mus. II. 84, ed. L. Kalmár in *Musica rinata*, 7 (Budapest, 1965). An even earlier divertimento for two clarinets and two horns, written for Bratislava in 1762, is lost.

10 Dwight Blazin, 'The two versions of Mozart's Divertimento K.113', *Music and Letters*, 73

(1992), pp. 32–47, including an illustration from the Michael Haydn divertimento. See also 'Correspondence', in *Music and Letters*, 74 (1993), pp. 485–7.

11 Notwithstanding Blazin, 'The two versions', pp. 41–2.

12 *The Letters of Mozart and his Family*, trans. Emily Anderson (London, 1938; rev. 2 vols., 1966), II, p. 638.

13 *Ibid.*, II, pp. 565–6.

14 Weston, *Clarinet Virtuosi of the Past*, p. 34.

15 These are the four sizes noted by Thomas Attwood during his studies with Mozart. See *Neue Mozart-Ausgabe* X/30/1, *Attwood-Studien*, p. 157.

16 Kingdon-Ward, 'Mozart's clarinettist'; Pisarowitz, "Müasst ma nix in übel aufnehma", Beitragsversuch zu einer Gebrüder-Stadler-Biographie'; Weston, *Clarinet Virtuosi of the Past*; and Poulin, *The Basset Clarinet of Anton Stadler and its Music*, 'The basset clarinet of Anton Stadler', and 'A report on new information regarding Stadler's concert tour of Europe and two early examples of the basset clarinet'.

17 Poulin, 'The basset clarinet of Anton Stadler', p. 69, citing F. Bertuch, 'Wiener Kunstnachrichten', *Journal des Luxus und der Moden*, 16 (October 1801), pp. 543–4.

18 Extant in the *Fürstlich Oettingen-Wallerstein'sche Bibliothek und Kunstsammlung*: cited by Poulin, 'The basset clarinet of Anton Stadler'. See also Poulin, 'A little-known letter of Anton Stadler', *Music and Letters*, 49 (1988), pp. 49–56.

19 Poulin, 'The basset clarinet of Anton Stadler', p. 69.

20 Gerber, *Historisch-biographisches Lexicon der Tonkünstler*, II, p. 556. Entries from the records of the Hoftheater include C clarinets with B joints (1782–3) for the Stadler brothers, two new clarinets with the usual *corps de rechange* ordered from Theodor Lotz (1784–5), another pair of boxwood clarinets from Lotz with the three usual *corps de rechange* (1785–6), and payment for extra duties and two newly manufactured cors anglais to the clarinettist Griesbacher (1794–5). See Roger Hellyer, 'Some documents relating to Viennese wind-instrument purchases, 1779–1837', *Galpin Society Journal*, 28 (1975), pp. 51–2.

21 It has been established that by 1788 Anton Stadler had assumed the first chair in the octet: *Staats-Schematismus* (Vienna, 1788), Austrian National Library.

22 Leeson and Whitwell, 'Concerning Mozart's Serenade for thirteen instruments'. Köchel erroneously believed that there were no competent clarinettists in Vienna before 1787.

23 Poulin, 'The basset clarinet of Anton Stadler', pp. 33–4.

24 *Magazin der Musik* (Hamburg, 1783), p. 179. Poulin, *The Basset Clarinet of Anton Stadler and its Music*, p. 25, noted that David was from Offenburg in Ortenau (near Strasbourg) and that Springer, David's pupil, was from Mláda Boleslav (Jungbunzlau, near Prague).

25 In 1791 H. Bossler noted the effectiveness of 'the so-called bass clarinets' as replacements for the bassoon. 'Berichtigungen und Zusätze zum den Musikalischen Almanachen auf die Jahre 1782, 1783, 1784', *Musikalische Korrespondenz der Teutschen Filarmonischen Gesellschaft für Jahr 1791*, eds. H. P. C. Bossler and J. F. Christmann, no. 6 (9 February 1791), cols. 41–2f.

26 *Mozart and the Masons* (London, 1982; rev. 1991), p. 20. Mozart's attitude to death is articulated in a celebrated letter of 4 April 1787 to his dying father.

27 The Master of the Crowned Hope Lodge was Count Johann Esterházy, a clarinet student of Stadler, according to the dedication of the latter's three solo *Caprices*.

28 According to Saam, *Das Bassetthorn*, Glöggl of Linz wrote in his *Lexicon* of 1812 that the basset horn was invented by a German in about 1760. Glöggl's father is said to have been the earliest basset horn teacher. Cramer merely stated that the instrument was believed to have been invented in Passau, probably as a result of the Mayrhofers' maker's stamp: ANT et MICH/ Mayrhofer/INVEN & ELABOR/PASSAVII.

29 P. 223. Koch describes a basset horn pitched in F.

30 *Magazin der Musik* (Hamburg, 1783), p. 654. Lotz, viola player and first clarinettist of Prince Joseph Batthay's orchestra, had performed for the Tonkünstler-Societät as early as 1772. He lived in Vienna from 1784, and in 1788 became 'kk Kammer Waldhorn- und Trompetenmacher'.

95

31 J. F. von Schönfeld, *Jahrbuch der Tonkunst von Wien und Prag* (1796), p. 58.
32 'Bassett-horn', *Allgemeine Encyclopädie der Wissenschaftlichen und der Kunst*, ed. J. S. Ersch and J. G. Grüber (Leipzig, 1822), VII, p. 49.
33 'The earliest basset horns', p. 10.
34 Prague, National Instrument Collection, National Museum 466E, dated 1796; Brussels, Musée du Conservatoire Royale de Musique 938, dated 1797.
35 One of the items (K41b) in Leopold Mozart's 1768 catalogue of his son's work to date includes 'many duets for basset horns', now lost.
36 Jeltsch, 'La clarinette de Mozart', p. 13.
37 Tyson, *Mozart: Studies of the Autograph Scores*, p. 19, notes that although Mozart entered K488 into his own Catalogue of Works on 2 March 1786, it had been begun a year or two earlier – probably between March 1784 and February 1785 – and that the original scoring contained parts for oboes rather than for clarinets.

3 The genesis and reception of the Concerto

1 Backofen, *Anweisung zur Klarinette*, p. 35.
2 Correspondence from Albert Rice. The concerto by Kozeluch at *A-Wn* 5853 has cadenzas for a normal clarinet and not – as claimed by Shackleton and Weston – for basset clarinet.
3 The first-movement cadenza is in Poulin, 'The basset clarinet of Anton Stadler', p. 79, with a misattribution of the concerto to the virtuoso Franz Tausch. Two *Eingänge* for the Romance and one for the Rondo allegretto are included in Lawson, 'The basset clarinet revived', p. 493.
4 Georg von Nissen, *Biographie W. A. Mozarts* (Leipzig, 1828), Anh. p. 17 No. 4.
5 Albrechtsberger makes a distinction between this convention and the use in clarinet parts of the term 'chalumeau' to qualify notation an octave higher than the sound.
6 Robert D. Levin, 'Das Klarinettenquintett B-Dur, KV Anh. 91/516c; ein Ergänzungversuch', *Mozart-Jahrbuch* (1968–70), p. 320, and the preface to his completion, published by Nagels Verlag (Cassel, 1970).
7 S. Newman, 'Mozart's G minor Quintet and its relationship to the G minor Symphony (K. 550)', *Music Review*, 17 (1956), p. 292. Mozart's clarinet quintet fragments are all reproduced in *NMA* VIII/19/2.
8 Tyson, *Mozart: Studies of the Autograph Scores*, pp. 341–2, note 28. Tyson also believes the fragment to have been originally complete.
9 C. F. Pohl, *Denkschrift aus Anlass des hundertjährigen Bestehens der Tonkünstler-Societät in Wien* (Vienna, 1871), p. 67. This obbligato was later performed on a conventional clarinet by such virtuosi as Heinrich Baermann, Crusell, Friedlowsky, Hermstedt and Willman. See Weston, *More Clarinet Virtuosi of the Past*, p. 357.
10 Discussed by Dieter Klöcker in his recording *Geistliche Arien für Sopran, konzertieren Klarinette und Orchester*, EMI IC/065–30 992 (1980).
11 Poulin, *The Basset Clarinet of Anton Stadler and its Music*, pp. 166–73.
12 Poulin, *The Basset Clarinet of Anton Stadler*, p. 42, notes that this account refers to the occasion of the arrival of the King of Naples, Ferdinand IV, to the court of Joseph II in Vienna. Stadler performed for this event, which was occasioned by the forthcoming marriage joining the Austrian Empire and Italy.
13 Deutsch, *Mozart: A Documentary Biography*, p. 365.
14 *The Letters of Mozart and his Family*, trans. E. Anderson (London, 1938; rev. 2 vols. 1966), II, p. 937.
15 Dazeley, 'The original text of Mozart's Clarinet Concerto', p. 171.
16 See especially Jiří Kratochvíl, 'Betrachtungen über die Urfassung des Konzerts für Klarinette und des Quintetts für Klarinette und Streicher von W. A. Mozarts', *Internationale Konferenz über das Leben und Werk W. A. Mozarts* (Prague, 1956), pp. 262–71; and 'Ist die heute gebrauchliche Fassung des Klarinettenkonzerts und des Klarinettenquintetts von Mozart

authentisch?', *Beiträge zur Musikwissenschaft*, 2 (1960), pp. 27–34; see also Gerhard Croll and Kurt Birsak, 'Anton Stadler's "Bassettklarinette" und das "Stadler-Quintett KV581"', *Österreichische Musikzeitung*, 24 (1969), pp. 3–11.

17 'Fragment eines Klarinetten-Quintetts von W. A. Mozart', *Zeitschrift für Musikwissenschaft*, 13 (1930–1), p. 221.

18 *NMA* VIII/19/2, p. xviii, has a facsimile of the passage, but does not reproduce these clefs in the text.

19 Poulin, 'A report on new information', p. 948; Tyson, *Mozart: Studies of the Autograph Scores.*

20 For example, Backofen (Concertante for two clarinets), Spohr (Octet, Concerto no. 4) Schumann (*Phantasiestücke*) and Brahms (Trio and Quintet).

21 Much of the following discussion of this complex area is indebted to Steblin, *A History of Key Characteristics in the Eighteenth and Early Nineteenth Centuries.*

22 *Observations sur notre instinct pour la musique* (Paris, 1754), translated by Steblin, *ibid.*, p. 104.

23 Translated by Steblin, *ibid.*, p. 140.

24 This distinction is discussed in *NMA* II/5/18, p. XIX, though in many editions the music for B clarinet has been transposed for A without further comment.

25 Deutsch, *Mozart: a Documentary Biography*, p. 393.

26 H. C. Robbins Landon, *1791: Mozart's Final Year* (London, 1988), p. 33.

27 P. Branscombe, *Die Zauberflöte* (Cambridge, 1991), pp. 137–8.

28 According to Weston, *Clarinet Virtuosi of the Past*, p. 55, the Stadlers played in a concert in Vienna in mid-September, in which Salieri was the conductor and the singers Cavalieri and Calvesi.

29 *The Letters of Mozart and his Family*, ed. Anderson, II, p. 967.

30 Hess, 'Die ursprüngliche Gestalt des Klarinettenkonzertes, KV622', pp. 18–30.

31 Gerber, *Historisch-biographisches Lexicon der Tonkünstler*, I, p. 824; Gottfried Weber, 'Über Clarinett und Bassetthorn', *Cäcilia*, 11 (1829), pp. 53ff.

32 The Viennese clarinettist Rudolf Jettel (who recorded the work in 1952) reported that his teacher Victor Polatschek (1889–1948) frequently alluded to remarks about the Concerto that were attributed to both Stadler and Mozart; according to Jettel, he possessed a handwritten copy of the Concerto that possibly belonged to one of Stadler's students. See Etheridge, *Mozart's Clarinet Concerto*, p. 129. Polatschek was also the teacher of the celebrated Mozart interpreter Leopold Wlach.

33 We may note in passing an earlier instance of different clarinets being sanctioned for alternative versions of a single piece, dictated by pragmatic considerations. For the sake of the singer, Mozart permitted 'Mi tradi' in *Don Giovanni* to be sung in D major (with obbligato A clarinet) rather than Eb (with Bb clarinet).

34 Private correspondence with the author, 17 January 1995.

35 Tyson, *Mozart: Studies of the Autograph Scores*, p. 35.

36 P. 147, note 47.

37 Weston, *Clarinet Virtuosi of the Past*, p. 55.

38 Poulin, 'An updated report', discovered that the second Warsaw concert included a clarinet concerto, together with a rondo and some variations. The programme opened with the second movement of a 'National Symphony' by the Czech composer Jan David Holland (1746–1826), based on 'elements of Polish Folk Music', and closed with 'some new Polish dances' performed by 'the Russian Orchestra having 130 members'. The Viennese pianist/composer Joseph Woelff (possibly Stadler's travelling companion) also played an unidentified piano concerto.

39 Poulin, 'An updated report', notes that Stadler stopped at Vilnius and possibly other Baltic cities in 1793. See Antoni Miller, *Teatr Polski i Muzyka na Litwie, 1745–1865* (Wilno [Vilnius], 1936), pp. 11 and 58.

40 Ed. J. F. Reichardt and F. A. Münzen, 15 (1792), p. 118.

41 'The first documented performance of the Mozart Clarinet Concerto or Stadler in Riga' delivered at the 1994 Chicago Clarinet Congress and reported in *The Clarinet*, 22/1 (1994),

p. 42. Poulin also discovered that the Riga concerts included a concerto of Stadler's own composition, a work otherwise unknown.

42 The opening bars of this version are reproduced in *Early Music*, 15 (1987), pp. 494–6, together with a later virtuoso passage (from bars 117 to 119), illustrating a four-octave scale from *c* to *c''''*.

43 Weston, *Clarinet Virtuosi of the Past*, p. 55, and Poulin, 'An updated report', p. 26.

44 *Clarinet Virtuosi of the Past*, p. 56.

45 Stadler died at the house of his young mistress, Friderika Kabel, leaving a wife Franciska and two sons Michael and Anton, jr.

46 Ernst Hess, 'Anton Stadler's "Musick Plan"', pp. 37–54.

47 Inventory and valuation of Mozart's estate in Deutsch, *Mozart: a Documentary Biography*, p. 585.

48 In Einstein's foreword (p. XXVI) to his edition of Köchel's catalogue, he suggests that the Concerto autograph may possibly have been one of the eight Mozart manuscripts which Constanze sold to the King of Prussia shortly after Mozart's death.

49 'Die ursprüngliche Gestalt der Klarinettenkonzertes', pp. 18–30.

50 Poulin, *The Basset Clarinet of Anton Stadler*, p. 182, also draws attention to a further reference to *AMZ* 1802 in the *Register zu den ersten zwanzig Jahrgängen der Allgemeine Musikalischen Zeitung, 1798–1818* (Leipzig, 1818), p. 123.

51 *More Clarinet Virtuosi of the Past* (London, 1977), p. 353.

52 Oscar Street, 'The clarinet and its music', p. 95.

53 Draper made a further recording of the Adagio alone in 1932. At this period, Dreisbach also recorded this movement, whilst di Caprio recorded the Allegro with piano accompaniment.

54 Other eminent European interpreters during the 1930s included Louis Cahuzac: see Weston, *More Clarinet Virtuosi of the Past*, p. 64.

55 English translation by Hilda Morris, revised Anthony Baines as *The Clarinet* (London, 1968).

56 *Essays in Musical Analysis*, VI (London, 1939), pp. 27–8. However, Tovey realised that an extended clarinet must have been used in *La clemenza di Tito*, though he writes that 'the history of this special instrument is unknown'.

57 Graham Melville-Mason, correspondence in *Clarinet and Saxophone*, 10/3 (1985), p. 22.

4 Stadler's clarinet and its revival

1 Ross, *A Comprehensive Performance Project in Clarinet Literature*, pp. 251–2. Tauber's surviving A clarinet is illustrated in *Early Music*, 15 (1987), p. 499.

2 See Hoeprich, 'Clarinet reed position in the 18th century'.

3 A five-keyed clarinet by Griesbacher is illustrated in Birsak, *Die Klarinette: Eine Kulturgeschichte*, pl. 11.

4 Gerber in 1812 (*Neues historisch-biographisches Lexicon*, I, 9. 911) described the workshop ('Dolegschy') as making the best oboes, flutes and bassoons in the whole of Bohemia. See William Waterhouse, *The New Langwill Index* (London, 1993), p. 92.

5 See Lawson, 'The basset clarinet revived', p. 497.

6 Illustrated in Brymer, *Clarinet*, fig. 9. An 8-keyed basset horn by F. Jäger of Carlsbad (CS-Prague Nat. Mus. 364E) resembles the Strobach in design.

7 'Wiener Kunstnachrichten', *Journal des Luxus und Moden*, 16 (October 1801), pp. 543–4. The passage was abbreviated and paraphrased by J. Schwaldopler, *Historisches Taschenbuch* (Vienna, 1805), and by Gerber, *Neues historisch-biographisches Lexicon der Tonkünstler*; both authors corrected Bertuch's almost certainly misprinted 'querrippe' ('lateral ridge') to the more familiar 'querpipe' ('transverse pipe').

8 Neisze and Leipzig, 1834.

9 Frankfurt, 1855.

10 Poulin, *The Basset Clarinet of Anton Stadler*, p. 188.

11 Unlike the other basset clarinets mentioned above, the Eisenbrandt has a fully chromatic extension. Poulin's publications continue (*Journal of the American Musical Instrument Society*, 1996) with an illustration of the engraving of Stadler's clarinet and further details of his repertoire and the names of clarinettists with whom he played.

12 A description of the letter appears in the antiquarian Hans Schneider's Katalog Nr 308 (Tutzing) of autographs of musicians, p. 76; I am grateful for this information to William Waterhouse. No evidence has surfaced as to whether Stadler actually played in Bremen.

13 The page (1174) bearing Scholl's advertisement is reproduced by Ross, *A Comprehensive Performance Project*, p. 271. He had taken over Lotz's workshop in 1792.

14 Bischoff finds a mention in the second of Backofen's clarinet tutors (1824).

15 Poulin, 'A report on new information', pp. 951–2. The other basset clarinet identified in her article, by Joseph Ziegler, is in fact a basset horn.

16 Eduard Hanslick, *Geschichte des Concertwesens in Wien* (Vienna, 1869), p. 118; Hermann Mendel, *Musicalisches Conversations-Lexicon* (Berlin, 1878), articles 'Stadler' and 'Clarinette'.

17 Rees-Davies, 'The Mozart Clarinet Concerto on record'.

18 Etheridge, *Mozart's Clarinet Concerto: the Clarinetist's View*.

19 The list was limited to the instruments commissioned by international figures (Kostohryz, Stalder, Hacker and Deinzer); by this time a number of other clarinettists owned extended instruments.

20 Kroll, *The Clarinet*, fig. 27.

21 'Anton Stadlers "Bassettklarinette" und das "Stadler-Quintett" KV 581. Versuch einer Anwendung', *Österreichische Musikzeitschrift*, 24/1 (January 1969), pp. 4, 5, 7.

22 Hacker, 'Mozart and the basset clarinet', p. 362. The instrument is also illustrated in Brymer, *Clarinet*, fig. 8. Planas extended a B♭ clarinet for Hacker shortly afterwards.

23 This instrument is illustrated in Lawson, 'The basset clarinet revived', fig. 6, and in Jeltsch, 'La clarinette de Mozart', p. 20.

24 E.g. Eric Hoeprich in an instrument of his own manufacture used for his 1985 recording (Philips 420 242). The author's basset clarinet, made by Daniel Bangham in 1988 and used for the recording Nimbus NI5228, incorporates a curved barrel and slight angle between joints, resembling the anonymous instrument listed as no. 5 in Appendix 2.

25 Illustrated in Lawson, 'The basset clarinet revived', fig. 5.

26 Illustrated in Birsak, *Die Klarinette: Eine Kulturgeschichte*, fig. 21.

5 Mozart's original text

1 'Betrachtungen über die Urfassung des Konzerts für Klarinette und des Quintetts für Klarinette und Streicher von W. A. Mozart', *Internationaler Konferenz über das Leben und Werk W. A. Mozarts* (Prague, 1956), pp. 262–71; 'Ist die heute gebrauchliche Fassung des Klarinettenkonzerts und des Klarinettenquintetts von Mozart authentisch?' *Beitrage zur Musikwissenschaft*, 2 (1960), pp. 27–34; 'Otázka puvodniho zneni Mozartova Koncertu pro Klarinet a Kvintetu pro Klarinet a smyce', *Hudebni věda* (1967), pp. 44–70. Kratochvíl was responsible for the reconstructed text of the Concerto in the 1951 performance.

2 'Die ursprüngliche Gestalt des Klarinettenkonzertes', pp. 18–30.

3 'Mozart and the basset clarinet', pp. 359–62.

4 Its associated piano reduction has a clarinet part which contrives usefully to incorporate both basset and normal A clarinet solo lines as alternatives.

5 *NMA Kritischer Bericht* V/14/4 (Cassel, 1982).

6 As explained in the preface, in the following discussion the abbreviation 1/91 indicates first movement, bar 91, etc. The term 'baritone' here and in following contexts denotes the lower part of the chalumeau register extending into the basset area.

7 *W. A. Mozart*, III, p. 296, note 48.

8 E.g. Dieter Klöcker in his recording of the Concerto on the normal A clarinet for Novalis

150 061–2 (1990): 'I find it deplorable that such minor matters as the appropriate type of solo instrument have become more important today than the actual work itself'.
9 Gervase de Peyer in an interview for *Clarinet & Saxophone*, 12/1 (1987), p. 34.

6 Design and structure

1 Arthur Hutchings, *A Companion to Mozart's Piano Concertos* (Oxford, 1948), p. 3.
2 Tyson, *Mozart: Studies of the Autograph Scores*, p. 252.

7 Performance practice

1 Robert Philip, *Early Recordings and Musical Style* (Cambridge, 1992), p. 240.
2 Neal Zaslaw, *Mozart Symphonies* (Oxford, 1989), pp. 508–9.
3 Louis Spohr, *Violinschule* (Vienna, [1832]), p. 179.
4 Türk, *Klavierschule* (Leipzig and Halle, 1789), translated by Raymond H. Haggh as *School of Clavier Playing* (Lincoln, NB, and London, 1982), pp. 360–1.
5 Türk, *ibid.*, pp. 310–11.
6 *Ibid.*, p. 313, including material from his 1802 edition.
7 Koch, *Musikalisches Lexicon* (Frankfurt, 1802/*R*1964), p. 929.
8 Reprinted in the 1959 edition by Karl Heinz Fuessl for the International Music Corporation.
9 Breitkopf and Härtel no. 2532, reproduced in Colin Lawson, 'Busoni's cadenza for the Mozart Clarinet Concerto', *The Clarinet*, 8/4 (1981), pp. 14–17.
10 The material is reproduced and discussed by Colin Lawson, 'Krticka's cadenzas for the Mozart Clarinet Concerto', *The Clarinet*, 9/2 (1982), pp. 35–7.
11 Ibert's two virtuoso and uninhibited cadenzas for Mozart's Bassoon Concerto were published by Leduc in 1937. See Colin Lawson, 'Ibert's cadenzas for the Mozart Clarinet Concerto', *The Clarinet*, 9/1 (1981), pp. 22–3.
12 As noted by Etheridge, *Mozart's Clarinet Concerto: the Clarinetist's View*, p. 146, Delécluse's own recording of the Concerto prefers the conventional linking passage from the Quintet, rather than the cadenza for the Adagio supplied by Ibert.
13 This was the principal source for the edition by Franz Giegling (Cassel, 1981) for the *NMA* V/14/3.
14 Cf. *NMA* V/14/4, p. XI.
15 Use of a keyboard instrument in orchestral music was at this time gradually being confined to vocal music. This was, for example, the situation found by Spohr at his arrival in Gotha in 1805. See Clive Brown, *Louis Spohr: a Critical Biography* (Cambridge, 1984), p. 36.

Appendix 2

1 Nos. 4–6 have a *corps de rechange* in B♭.
2 Doleisch Y1 does not exist.
3 *Fl.* Beraun, near Prague.
4 Recently stolen.
5 This instrument is lost.
6 Nos. 13, 14, 23, 24 and 25 have a key for low E♭.
7 Nos. 1 and 2 are early sickle-shaped.
8 Strobach style, eight-keyed.

Select bibliography

Adlung, J., *Anleitung zu der Musikalischen Gelahrtheit* (Erfurt, 1758)

Albrechtsberger, J. G., *Gründlicher Anweisung zur Composition* (Leipzig, 1790)

Bach, C. P. E., *Versuch über die wahre Art das Clavier zu spielen*, 2 vols. (Berlin, 1753–62), trans. W. J. Mitchell as *Essay on the True Art of Playing Keyboard Instruments* (New York, 1949)

Backofen, J. G. H., *Anweisung zur Klarinette, nebst einer kurzen abhandlung über das Bassett-Horn* (Leipzig, *c*. 1803 R1986)

Baines, A., *Woodwind Instruments and their History* (London, 1957; 3rd edn, 1967/ R1991)

Becker, H., 'Zur Geschichte der Klarinette im 18. Jahrhundert', *Die Musikforschung*, 8 (1955), pp. 271–92

Birsak, K., *Die Holzblasinstrumente im Salzburger Museo Carolino Augusteum* (Salzburg, 1973)

Die Klarinette: Eine Kulturgeschichte (Buchloe, 1992), Eng. trans. G. Schamberger (1994)

'Salzburg, Mozart und die Klarinette', *Mitteilungen der Internationalen Stiftung Mozarteum*, 33 (1985), pp. 40–7

Boese, H., *Die Klarinette als Soloinstrument in der Musik der Mannheimer Schule* (Dresden, 1940)

Bonanni, F., *Gabinetto armonico* (Rome, 1722)

Brymer, J., *Clarinet* (London, 1976)

Croll, G., and Birsak, K., 'Anton Stadlers "Bassettklarinette" und das "Stadler-Quintett" KV 581: Versuch einer Anwendung', *Österreichische Musikzeitschrift*, 24/1 (1969), pp. 3–11

Croll, G., 'Diskussion "Horn", "Klarinette" und "Bassettklarinett"', *Mozart-Jahrbuch* (1968–70), pp. 27–9

Dazeley, G., 'The original text of Mozart's Clarinet Concerto', *Music Review*, 9 (1948), pp. 166–72

Deutsch, O. E., *Mozart: a Documentary Biography* (Eng. trans. 1965; suppl. edn, 1978)

Doppelmayr, J. G., *Historische Nachricht von den Nürnbergischen Mathematicis und Künstlern* (Nuremberg, 1730)

Einstein, A., *Mozart: his Character, his Work* (Eng. trans. New York, 1945)

Eppelsheim, J., 'Bassetthorn-Studien', *Studia organologica: Festschrift für John Henry van der Meer zu seinem fünfundsechzigsten Geburtstag*, ed. F. Hellwig (Tutzing, 1987), pp. 69–125

'Das Denner-Chalumeau des Bayerischen Nationalmuseums', *Die Musikforschung*, 26 (1973), pp. 498–500

Etheridge, D., *Mozart's Clarinet Concerto: the Clarinetist's View* (Gretna, LA, 1983)

Gerber, E. L., *Historisch-biographisches Lexicon der Tonkünstler* (Leipzig, 1790–92/ R1977)

Neues historisch-biographisches Lexicon der Tonkünstler (Leipzig, 1812–14/R1966)

Gradenwitz, P., 'The beginnings of clarinet literature: notes on a clarinet concerto by Joh. Stamitz', *Music and Letters*, 17 (1936), pp. 145–50

Hacker, A., 'Mozart and the basset clarinet', *Musical Times*, 110 (1969), pp. 359–62

Haskell, H., *The Early Music Revival* (London, 1988)

Hess, E., 'Anton Stadler's "Musick Plan"', *Mozart-Jahrbuch* (1962), pp. 37–54

'Die ursprüngliche Gestalt des Klarinettenkonzerts KV622', *Mozart-Jahrbuch* (1967), pp. 18–30

Hoeprich, T. E., 'Clarinet reed position in the 18th century', *Early Music*, 12 (1984), pp. 49–55

Jeltsch, J., 'La clarinette de Mozart', *Crescendo: Le Magazine de la musique ancienne*, 34 (1990), pp. 12–24

Kingdon-Ward, M., 'Mozart's clarinettist', *Monthly Musical Record* (January 1955), pp. 21–34

Koch, H. C., *Musikalisches Lexicon* (Offenbach, 1802/R1964)

Kroll, O., *Die Klarinette* (Cassel, 1965), trans. H. Morris as *The Clarinet*, ed. A. Baines (London, 1968)

Langwill, L. G., *An Index of Musical Woodwind Makers* (Edinburgh, 1960; rev., enlarged 6th edn, 1980), rev. W. Waterhouse as *The New Langwill Index* (London, 1993)

Lawson, C., 'The authentic clarinet: tone and tonality', *Musical Times*, 124 (1983), pp. 357–8

'The basset clarinet revived', *Early Music*, 15 (1987), pp. 487–501

(ed.) *The Cambridge Companion to the Clarinet* (Cambridge, 1995)

The Chalumeau in Eighteenth-Century Music (Ann Arbor, 1981)

Leeson, D. N., and Whitwell, D., 'Concerning Mozart's Serenade for thirteen instruments, KV 361 (370ª)', *Mozart-Jahrbuch* (1976–7), pp. 97–130

Mozart, L., *Versuch einer gründlichen Violinschule* (Augsburg, 1756/R1976; trans. E. Knocker, 1948)

Newhill, J. P., *The Basset-Horn and its Music* (Sale, 1983, rev. edn, 1986)

'The contribution of the Mannheim School to clarinet literature', *Music Review*, 10 (1979), pp. 90–122

Nickel, E., *Die Holzblasinstrumentenbau in der freien Reichsstadt Nürnberg* (Munich, 1971)

Philip, R., *Early Recordings and Musical Style* (Cambridge, 1992)

Pisarowitz, K. M., '"Müasst ma nix in übel aufnehma...", Beitragsversuche zu einer Gebrüder-Stadler-Biographie', *Mitteilungen der Internationalen Stiftung Mozarteum*, 19 (1971), pp. 29–33

Poulin, P. L., 'A report on new information regarding Stadler's concert tour of Europe and two early examples of the basset clarinet', *Mozart-Jahrbuch* (1991), pp. 946–55

'An updated report on new information regarding Stadler's concert tour of Europe and two early examples of the basset clarinet', *The Clarinet*, 22/2 (1995), pp. 24–8

'The basset clarinet of Anton Stadler', *College Music Symposium*, 22 (1982), pp. 67–82

The Basset Clarinet of Anton Stadler and its Music, diss. (University of Rochester, NY, 1977)

Procházka, R., *Mozart in Prag* (Prague, 1892)

Quantz, J. J., *Versuch einer Anweisung die Flöte traversiere zu spielen* (Berlin, 1752; 3rd edn, 1789/*R*1953), trans. E. R. Reilly as *On Playing the Flute* (London and New York, 1966)

Rees-Davies, J., *Bibliography of the Early Clarinet* (Brighton, 1986)

'The Mozart Clarinet Concerto on record', *Clarinet & Saxophone*, 14/4 (1989), pp. 12–14

Reich, Willi, 'Bermerkungen zu Mozarts Klarinettenkonzert', *Zeitschrift für Musikwissenschaft*, 15 (1932–3), pp. 276–8

Rendall, F. G., *The Clarinet* (London, 1954; rev. 3rd edn by P. Bate, 1971)

Rice, A. R., 'Clarinet fingering charts, 1732–1816', *Galpin Society Journal*, 37 (1984), pp. 16–41

The Baroque Clarinet (Oxford, 1992)

'The clarinette d'amour and basset horn', *Galpin Society Journal*, 39 (1986), pp. 97–124

Ross, D., *A Comprehensive Performance Project in Clarinet Literature with an Organological Study of the Development of the Clarinet in the Eighteenth Century*, DMA thesis (University of Iowa, 1985)

Saam, J., *Das Bassetthorn* (Mainz, 1971)

Schink, J. F., *Litterarische Fragmente* (Graz, 1785)

Schmid, E. F., 'Gluck–Starzer–Mozart', *Zeitschrift für Musik*, 104 (1937), pp. 1198–209

Schönfeld, J. F. von, *Jahrbuch der Tonkunst von Wien und Prag* (Vienna, 1796/*R*1976)

Schubart, C. F. D., *Ideen zu einer Ästhetik der Tonkunst* (Vienna, 1806/*R*1969)

Shackleton, N., 'The earliest basset horns', *Galpin Society Journal*, 40 (1987), pp. 2–23

Steblin, R., *A History of Key Characteristics in the Eighteenth and Early Nineteenth Centuries* (Ann Arbor, 1983)

Street, O. W., 'The clarinet and its music', *Proceedings of the Musical Association*, 42 (1915–16), pp. 89–115

Tenschert, R., 'Fragment eines Klarinetten-Quintetts von W. A. Mozart', *Zeitschrift für Musikwissenschaft*, 13 (1930–1), pp. 218–22

Türk, D. G., *Klavierschule* (Leipzig and Halle, 1789), trans. Raymond H. Haggh as *School of Clavier Playing* (Lincoln, NB, and London, 1982)

Tyson, A., *Mozart: Studies of the Autograph Scores* (London, 1987)

Weston, P., *Clarinet Virtuosi of the Past* (London, 1971)

More Clarinet Virtuosi of the Past (London, 1977)

Whewell, M., 'Mozart's basset horn trios', *Musical Times*, 103 (1962), p. 19

Young, P. T., *4900 Historical Woodwind Instruments: an Inventory of 200 Makers in International Collections* (London, 1993)

Index